What Happens When God Says,
"Let There Be...!"

What Happens When God Says, "Let There Be...!"

Pastor Dollie Sherman

EJF PUBLISHING HOUSE
Chicago, Illinois

Pastor Dollie Sherman/EJF PUBLISHING HOUSE
www.dollieshermanministries.com

Publisher's Note: For purposes of sharing Names, characters, places, and incidents are a product of the author's imagination. Locales and public names are sometimes used for atmospheric purposes. Any resemblance to actual people, living or dead, or to businesses, ministries, churches, companies, events, institutions, or locales is completely coincidental.

Book Cover David Dickerson Photo & Design
Website www.daviddickersonphotoanddesign.com

Book Interior Design EJF Publishing House

What Happens When God Says, "Let There Be…!"/Pastor Dollie Sherman -- 1st ed.
ISBN 978-1-7368985-0-5

EJF PUBLISHING HOUSE

Chicago, Illinois

Contents

Dedication

This book is dedicated to my mother and father (now deceased), as well as, to my husband who loved me in my infant stages of womanhood. To my daughter, son, granddaughter, grandsons, sisters, brothers, sisters-in-laws, goddaughters, godsons, nieces, nephews, cousins, friends, girlfriends, Sunday school teacher, all who have known me in the past, and those who will know me in the future, this book is dedicated to you, too.

I also want to acknowledge Apostle Donald Alford, Pastors Gloria Alford and DeAndre Patterson, who nurtured me spiritually when I needed it most, and Minister Paulette Hill, who has seen me in the worst of times but never judged or exposed me. To all the mentors and mothers, who loved and coached me along the way, I am forever grateful. Lady Desiree Fleming, thank you for taking the time to be a midwife to a midwife, and for helping me to push this book out of my loins.

Lastly, to any person who feels that your life was created without meaning, believes your scars will never heal, and is paralyzed by negative words, this book is for you. In your eyes you see flaws, but God, who created you in His image, sees victories. This book is written to encourage you to embrace who you are and know that you are God's designer original.

Foreword

Encouraging, empowering, and inspiring! This book is a MUST read! By the grace of God and the spirit of tenacity, you too, can over-come the impediments and the vicissitudes of life. You change the trajectory of your destiny and become the person God foreordained you to be before the foundation of the world. Never allow your circumstances to speak louder than the word that God has spoken concerning you. Despite your flaws, you can flourish and tri-umph over your trials and evolve into exactly who God created you to be. You will appreciate Pastor Dollie Sherman's transparency and be motivated to persevere and make progression in your own life as you read this dynamic book.

Dr. Joyce Thornton, Texas

Foreword

God has truly used Pastor Dollie to reveal to us the heartbeat of God for mankind. This revelation does not come from the ivory tower but from her own life experiences. Being able to share such a powerful revelation that no matter how broken you become or what life challenges you with, God has a spoken word over your life that will bring you from despair to your destiny! Pastor Dollie's valuable nuggets in this book will encourage you to become all that God has ordained you to be.

Pastor Gwen Porter, Chicago, Illinois

Our Mother, Dollie Sherman

Watching her endure and persevere
through life's tribulations,
We saw the strength a woman can possess.
Adhering to her words of guidance,
We experienced the wisdom of a mother.
Just when we thought she'd given her all
....here comes more.

Proverbs 31:31: Honor her for all that her
hands have done, and let her works bring
her praise at the city gate.

Luster P. Johnson & April Sherman

What Happens When God Says, "Let There Be...!"

INTRODUCTION

What Happens When God Says, "Let There Be . . . !"
"My Life Unfolded"

I have been inspired to write this book by the Holy Spirit. He has commanded me to tell the world and all who read it to remember the words spoken by God over two thousand years ago and that His Word will stand forever and ever.

God spoke in the book of Genesis 1:3, "And God said, Let there be light: and there was light." When these words were uttered by the Creator, all things came into existence by Him. All things were already created in Him in the beginning. Before the foundation of the world all things were already in Him. The Lord spoke to me concerning my own beginning. I know He spoke to me because the proof is in the book of Jeremiah, chapter 1, "Before I formed thee in the belly I knew thee, and I ordained thee a prophet unto the nations. Then said I, Ah, Lord God! Behold, I cannot speak: for I am a child. But the Lord said unto me say not, that thou are a child: for thou shalt go to all that I shall send thee, and whatsoever I command thee thou shalt speak." (Jer. 1:5-6)

Well, my life story is not the glamourous story most people would want to read about. But it is the story of when God spoke His word over me and I know His word shall not return unto Him void. (Isaiah 55:11) In this book I share my story including the character flaws that I was sure would disqualify me from service in the kingdom of God. Unfortunately, too many of us see ourselves as flawed and useful. However, God does not see us the way we do. He created us in His image and He created us perfect and whole. There are no flaws in the image of God. The flaws came when disobedience entered the Garden of Eden as a result of sin. Since then, our character has become flawed and our bloodline tainted. But there is hope in the midst of the Garden to cleanse and restore humanity to its original state. Oh! But it does not stop there. Revelation 13:8 declares that Jesus Christ was "the Lamb slain from the foundation of the world." It is he who prepares my defense papers restoring every character flaw and tainted bloodline. When Jesus was slain before anything was created on earth, before sin entered the garden, His blood hung there waiting to cover me, waiting to justify me, waiting to cleanse me. Before I go into that, I want to stress that when God speaks, all creation must hear, listen, and obey.

The book of Genesis is known as the beginning. In Genesis God is known as *Elohim*. This name only occurs in the Hebrew and in no other ancient Semitic language. It's interesting that the masculine plural ending does not mean "gods" when referring to the true God of Israel. The name is mainly used with singular verb forms and with adjectives and pronouns in the singular (e.g., Genesis 1:26). But when we consider the Hashalush Hakadosh (Trinity), the form indeed allows for the plurality within the Godhead.

God (Elohim) spoke into existence all creation because it was already in His being--in His thoughts and breath. He already had the pattern laid out in His mind. God was already pregnant with the earth and mankind within Him. The Holy Ghost and Jesus are Master Architects on the scene ready to carry out every Word that proceeds out of the mouth of God. Therefore, Genesis is the time of birthing. In Genesis 1:26, we read, "And God said, Let us make man in our image, after our likeness: and let them have dominion over the fish of the sea, and over all the earth, and over every creeping thing that creepeth upon the earth." This is the plural of Elohim speaking. God had to be Elohim (plural) because we were within Him. I need a praise break right there. The text goes on to read: "So God (Elohim) created man in his own image, in the image of God created he him; male and female created he them." (Gen 1:27).

When God said "let us make man," everything about us was shaped, formed and fashioned. That thing that was already in God was about to manifest itself. The birthing was taking place and the earth was his birthing stool. The birthing stool, mourning bench, and everything we needed was already provided for us. But, that's for another book.

Everything that God spoke in the first chapter of Genesis is still in its place today and forever more. Everything is still in its place because the Lord knew before the foundation of the world that man was going to blow it. This is the reason that in the book of Revelation we read that the Lamb was slain before the foundation of the world. (Revelation 13:8) I believe that Jesus' blood was suspended in a spiritual holding place until the time when sin entered into the garden of Eden. It reminded me of the oil that would not flow when Samuel was trying to anoint the sons of Jesse as King over Israel. The oil would not flow until God's choice, David, arrived. When David appeared before Samuel, the oil flowed like water. (I Samuel 16:12-13).

We should know that sin entered the world through Adam and Eve as a result of the schemes of the devil. Before that happened, God was not about to waste his Son's blood on an empty earth. The devil had no power to create anything, but he used his cunning to corrupt what God had made. Therefore, God kicked him out of heaven into outer darkness. But that is another story.

According to an online dictionary, *an embryo is an organism in its early stage of development, especially before it has reached a distinctly recognizable form.* After several weeks of growing inside a woman or animal, it starts to take on the shape of whatever it is to be!!! But, when God says, "Let it be," that thing has already taken its shape, form and fashion.

When God's creation manifested itself in the earth by His spoken word, He had already put inside of us a character. Our character is what determines how we respond to situations. God knew from the beginning of time how we would respond, act, to the different circumstances that come our way. So, God in his awesomeness had already put into motion by his word exactly what we would need to know and hear.

The definition of character is the mental and moral qualities distinctive to an individual. The seven pillars are honesty, courage, compassion, concern for the environment, integrity, knowledge, unselfishness, and trustworthiness. To me, these are good flesh fruits that we all should possess. And when we get filled with the Holy Ghost, we are called to walk in the spirit and demonstrate a certain fruit. This <u>fruit</u> of the Spirit is not plural but there are nine attributes. Love is the fruit of the spirit. Love is the fruit of the spirit. (More about this in chapter 3) Faith is one of the attributes of the fruit of the Spirit. One day before Bible Study, God posed a question to me: "Will your character reveal your faith? How will I handle criticism, rejection, and hatred?"

God knew in this life we would have choices. The choices we often make are not always the will of God for our lives. I know that the Lord prompted me to write this book because there are many of us out here who feel we cannot do what God has called us to do. We can't because we measure ourselves so many times against others. But God is saying, "I created you in my image, I created you perfect. I created you to be all that I need you to be."

Let me share with you just briefly some of my story. I was born in the Mississippi Delta, a very rural area. I grew up in an environment where there was love, peace, and laughter. We experienced great relationships, but we fell short in the education department and that impacted me. I noticed that whenever we would leave our comfort zone and visit another area of Mississippi, I realized that our dialect was different. We pronounced words differently. Some of our words would be chopped up so that we did not say the whole word as other people would normally pronounce them. Even though we were educated, English was not our greatest subject. There was no doubt that our speech was so different because of the environment we grew up in. Most of the parents did not have high levels of education. The most they knew was how to sign their name and maybe read at a third-grade level.

Living in an environment with people who are not so educated and who do not know how to properly pronounce their words definitely shaped my experience. People tend to be influenced by the environment they live in or come from, usually conforming to its negative or positive traits. For example, if you are in an environment where there is chaos, hatred and bitterness, there is a great chance it is going to impact you and influence the attitude you project. I am so grateful for the love, peace and hope that my family instilled in me. I learned how to respect myself and others, but I also realized I had to speak slowly as though I were memorizing a script. I had to try to speak the words without chopping them up and sometimes that was embarrassing. It was difficult because people would laugh at you if you couldn't speak as properly as they did. One of my older brothers had a really bad stutter when he talked. It reminded me of Moses who had a stutter, but was anointed. My brother sometimes was shy to speak in front of strangers because sometimes it took him sometimes to get his sentence out. His stutter was truly a thorn in his side.

Later on, I noticed again how my environment affected me when I moved and became an urban dweller. Living a few miles away from the inner city, I soon learned the way of urban speaking people. So if speaking is a learned behavior then I can change the way I talk by changing my environment, practicing what I say before I say it, and listening to others speak. It may seem like a minor issue but for someone who is self-conscious about their speech, it is pure hell and fear. It caused a person like me to go into a shell and become shy and intimidated with a low self-esteem. I used to be embarrassed to speak openly in conversation.

For those of us that have such flaws that we believe are God given, be encouraged. When God first created humans, he made people in His image and they had no flaws. Our flaws have come from our struggles in our environment after sin showed up. In my case, maybe I can't say the words as clearly as someone else can. I may even have a stutter like Moses, but Moses had a stutter and the anointing. My words may be urban slang, but it houses the anointing. The anointing is what delivers and sets free; it is the "Hammer of God." The anointing will break asunder any yoke and it comes with power and authority!

The words that God speaks to us will break any chains and remove anything that is holding you down. I had to start seeing myself as God sees me. But that does not mean I don't still have challenges on this journey. Although I was called from the beginning, I still have struggles but I praise God that He is there to help me overcome every hurdle I encounter on my journey.

I remember one day I was just sitting in my backyard and I began to reflect on the goodness of the Lord. I started thinking about how it all failed in the garden. Before sin entered the picture, everything was good. When God said, "Let there be, that BE was loaded with everything that was needed for existence. When God said to the Trinity," let us make man in our image" and then breathed the "ruach," breath of life into him, man became a living soul. Everything that Adam needed was downloaded into him! He was full of God's glory. I imagine that Adam was like a superhero. He could go down into the depths of the ocean and be able to breathe underwater. He had the ability to look at a whale and name it. Then he categorized it as the largest mammal in the waters. He called it a whale because he had the information already downloaded from God. Likewise, he could look at a shark and name it because he had all the information downloaded in him. He was hearing from God and he knew the language of heaven and earth. He would walk on land and see the lions and tigers and bears, oh my! All the while, he knew the distinctions of each of these animals. He could look up in the sky and see God's glory. He was so full of God's glory that he could look at the birds of the air and name the eagle, the crow, and the buzzard. He named the sparrow, duck, and chicken. He could do all of these amazing things because of the ability that was already downloaded in him.

Today God is saying that when He breathes "ruach" life into us, we have the ability to do everything that He calls us to do. The flaws that others and we ourselves identify are only an opportunity for God to show us that He paid it all and is able to restore us back into our rightful place. The Bible declares that "we shall have whatsoever we desire as long as we believe in faith, not wavering and asking nothing in amiss from his Word." (James 4:3 KJV).

There are things that have been spoken over your life at one time or another, some good and some bad. I learned that most of the time we believe the bad things people speak over our lives before we believe the good things God has spoken concerning our lives. God declares in His word that we are the head and not the tail; we are above and not beneath; we are the lenders and not the borrowers (Deuteronomy 28:12-13). It does not matter what someone else says concerning your life as long as you believe what God has spoken in his Word concerning you.

You have to take the initiative of being your own prophet and you have the Word of God to back you up. Jeremiah 1:5 states, "Before I formed thee in the belly I knew thee; and before thou camest forth out of the womb I sanctified thee and, I ordained thee a prophet unto the nations." We have already been ordained by God to prophesy into nations. However, we need to submit ourselves under spiritual authority so that you and your gift will have a spiritual covering in your ministry. A covering will give you guidance, train you, and cultivate your gift so that you can edify others and not bring chaos and destruction to lives. Submitting to spiritual authority will allow you to grow and be able to hear the Word of God and speak it in season and out of season.

Now if and when you hear negative things that can damage or alter your life, please remember this if you remember nothing else. God clearly tells us in Jeremiah 29:11, "For I know the thoughts that I think toward you, saith The Lord, thoughts of peace, and not of evil, to give you an expected end. God is giving us hope in our past, present, and future." Now, ain't that some good news?

I remember over thirty some years ago when fresh out of high school, I moved from my hometown in Tchula, Mississippi to Chicago. I had always wanted to move to Chicago with my cousins who had already dropped out of grammar school and moved there. Growing up in my mother's house, all my siblings were determined that I would be the one to break the "drop out cycle" in our family. My older siblings had dropped out to help make a living for the rest of us. I pause here to say thank you to them for their labor of love and for the sacrifices they made for me. My brothers and sisters hoovered over my life to make sure I would not be a statistic in the education field. My desire was truly to have an education. They welcomed me to their home each summer and paid me to babysit. Most of my nieces and nephews were just as big and old as I was. They helped me to work little summer jobs in the field with other youth. They allowed me to drive their cars with no driving license. They would sneak behind my back and tell my boyfriends, "this is my little sister and don't mess with her." They gave me money when my parents could not afford to. They made sure I had everything I needed when it came to paying for school trips, my class rings (my mother helped too) and my graduation. I hope I have made them proud by continuing my education so that I now hold two Bachelor's degrees and an Associate degree. I am currently working on my Master's degree. I realize that all glory and honor belongs to God.

Once I made it out of high school, my family took pride in that and finally allowed me to go to Chicago, Illinois with my cousins. My dad was not in agreement at all so in the middle of the night I had to sneak out from my home as a prisoner breaking out of jail. Truth be told, my father was afraid for his baby girl going so far away from him. My dad was the type of person who took pride in all his children sitting around the table feasting on Sundays and holidays. But, my mother often told him that there was something special about me, this child of theirs. Although she couldn't quite put her finger on it she knew I was different. I would often hear her telling my dad, "we can't keep her locked up in this small world. She is smart, educated and very inquisitive. Sooner or later we will have to allow her to spread her wings as the eagle. We cannot cage her or we may lose her to the unknown."

But, my dad, ever the protector, worried about me. "If something happened to her, how could I get there to help?"

My mom would say, "We have to trust the God that is in her. Let's tell her some of the do's and don'ts of life because if we try to keep her here, she will eventually die anyway or she will sneak away and we may never see her again."

But, my dad still was not convinced. So, plan B went into action. My dad went to bed early but my mother and I were late nighters. On the night my cousins were returning to Chicago, they came by to get me and away I went.

When I arrived in Chicago, I was disappointed to see the way my cousins lived. But, I had another friend who had moved to Chicago and she was a whole lot more stable than they were. Before I left home, my mother made sure that I had everybody's numbers. I am so glad that she did. The cousin I originally came to Chicago with was once my ace buddy. We did everything together. When you saw her, you saw me. The difference between us was that I had dreams of being somebody, dreams of helping people like my family and friends. Her plan was to quit school and make lots of money without an education.

I knew something was wrong the way she was thinking about the plans she had. Although she saw a lot of physical, mental abuse, and deaths, and was sure this was not going to happen to her, it did. Sadly, she got caught up in drugs, alcohol, and abuse. I am still believing God for a complete deliverance and healing for her.

I remember some of the older women living on the plantation would often say to us, "you are not gonna be anything because you are too hard headed." Today I know they were referring to us being disrespectful and disobedient. I realize now that we preferred to ignore our elders than listen to their counsel. Instead of listening to their reprimands, we began to keep our distance. Staying away from the older generations was not the best solution for our struggles. We needed the older, seasoned generations to help teach us wisdom, respect, and morals. So many of the younger people today are sorely missing this advice of the elders. After coming here to Chicago, Illinois I realized that my cousins and I were on two separate pages. I was determined to live out my goals and dreams while my cousin is caught up in the very things she said she would never do.

What Happens When God Says, "Let There Be...!"

CHAPTER 1

Do You Believe In Angels?
"The Devil is Not Short"

"Goodness and mercy shall follow me all the days of my life and I will dwell in the house of the Lord forever." (Psalms 23:6)

Do you believe in angels? This question no longer raises a thought in my mind. I don't need to read any books about it. I don't need to ask any questions or get anyone else's opinion about it for I have had a personal experience with God's guardian angel. I believe that we are all assigned a guardian angel to protect us until our destiny is fulfilled. God has our guardian angel protecting us even when we are not saved.

When I was a disobedient and hard-headed little girl, God still protected me. Jeremiah 1: 5 reminded me of the word of the Lord, "Before I formed you in the womb I knew you, before you were born, I set you apart . . ." God definitely had a future for me.

There was a time that I used to speak my mind or just tell a person off. I did not have a problem giving someone a piece of my mind especially since I was not filled with the Holy Ghost. But I thank God that Jesus had patience with Peter because he knew that one day Peter would become a Rock that He would embrace.

He is also calling me to be one of His own. In the Book of Matthew, chapter 16, verses 13 through 19, Jesus asked his disciples this question: "Who does man say that I am?" And they said, "Some say that thou art John the Baptist, some say Elijah and others, Jeremiah, or one of the prophets.

"*T*his is the true foundation of God's Church."

But then Jesus asked them, "Who do you say that I am?" Then Simon Peter answered and said, "Thou art the Christ, the son of the living God." And Jesus answered and said unto him, "Blessed art thou Simon bar Jonah for flesh and blood had not revealed it until you but my Father which is in Heaven. And I say unto you that thou art Peter and upon this Rock I will build my church and the gates of hell shall not prevail against it."

This is the true foundation of God's Church. Jesus did not say that he would build his church upon Peter, but upon the statement that Peter had made. Peter's name, *Petro*, means small stones. But Jesus said that he would build his church upon himself, *Petra*, which means Big Rock. Jesus is The Rock of Ages, the Ancient One. The demons he fought with then are the same demons we fight with today. Although we are in a different day, time, and era, the book of Revelation gives us the key to their destruction in the lake of fire. (Revelation 20:14)

My testimony about angels regards the angel that has been assigned to me. I hope and pray that this testimony about what happened will ease someone's mind. Hopefully, the anointing that will be upon this book will agree with your spirit so that unbelief and doubt will not be a hindrance to your faith. My prayer is that you can begin seeing and understanding the true manifestation of God's ministering angels.

The experience that I am about to share with you will give you a glimpse of the hedge of protection that God has surrounding each of us. Through this experience I often find myself praying to God to give my ministering angel strength and special charge over my life. Please understand me. I did not say that I pray to my angels but that I pray to God because Satan seeks to deceive some Christians if they are not careful. In 2 Corinthians 11:14, we read, "And no marvel; for Satan himself is transformed into an angel of light. Therefore it is no great thing if his ministers also be transformed as the ministers of righteousness; whose end shall be according to their works."

Satan ministering is not to protect you but to deceive you. They will show you the pleasures of this world but it will only last for a moment. They certainly will not show you the end there. I am not trying to be the expert on angels. Actually, I know very little about angels. All I know is what happened to me.

Earlier I shared about the time when I was talking to the Lord and telling him that I wanted to leave the plantation. I did not want to stay there all my life. I remember when my cousin, friends, and I would go

fishing. We would talk about leaving and going somewhere for the summer. During the summer, some children from families who were more well to do that lived
in town or in neighboring areas often would go away
on vacations. They would come back to school from
their summer vacations and our teachers would ask
everybody to share their experiences they had over the
summer break. Well, I would be in class listening to all
the stories about fantasy trips, the new clothes, and
the friends that they had made over the summer vacation.

      Our parents could not afford to send us away on
vacations. Neither were they about to trust anyone else
with their children for the whole summer that far from
home. As a result, my usual summer vacation was
working, fishing, and playing basketball. One year, I
decided that for the next summer I would be going
away. In the following months I began working to get
my plans in place.

      I was very smart in school and I could write let-
ters like an adult. I decided to write a letter to one of
my sisters-in-law who lived in Milwaukee, Wisconsin.
I made it seem like it was my mother asking her to let
me come up to Wisconsin. I always felt that I was one
of her favorite little sisters because her sisters and I
played together all the time. She was married to my
older brother. (Sadly, both are now deceased.) I wrote
her a letter like it was from my mother. The letter em-
phasized that I needed a summer experience I could
write about when I returned to school. I told her that
my mother and my brother were going to pay all the
expenses. Now this sister-in-law and my older brother
were separated but we always looked to her as our sis-

ter. Plus, she never had a daughter, so I was the daughter she never had. She had two sons. The oldest and I were close in age.

As it happened, I never heard back from her. In fact, the letter came back undelivered because no such person was at that address. When that letter came back, my heart was crushed. That had been my only hope of getting away for the summer. Now my mother could not read or write but she could count her money and sign her name. So I played a trick on her and pretended that my sister-in-law had written back. I put an old phone number in the letter like it was my sister's phone number although my sister-n-law's phone number was disconnected.

Early in May I started working on my bus fare. One of my older brothers would pay me to iron his clothes, polish his shoes, and take his clothes back and forth to the cleaners. I would braid little kids' hair for money. All the time, I was saving to purchase a one-way ticket to Milwaukee, Wisconsin. I expected to return home, but my plan was to ask my sister-in-law to send me back. I really was not running away to stay. I just wanted to experience a better summer.

On Friday, July 19, 1973, about two weeks before my scheduled trip to Milwaukee, a dark cloud hung heavy over our small community. The newscaster that morning had predicted a sunny day. But around noon, the gathering of dark clouds caused everyone to wonder if it was going to rain or storm. Then, we got a chilling phone call from a little town called Thornton, Mississippi. (Thornton is a topographic surname, which was given to a person who resided near a physical feature such as a hill, stream, church, or type of tree. In this case, the surname Thornton was originally from the Old English terms "thorn" meaning thorn bushes and "tun" meaning enclosure or town.)

It was during lunch time when my brother and some of his co-workers were on their way to Thornton to eat lunch. My brother was on the back of the pickup truck asleep. A man named 'Simon' was the driver. They were headed south, about to make a left turn heading into Thornton. Meanwhile, an 18-wheeler truck was headed northbound. Road work was being done on this particular stretch of highway 49. Three younger sons had snuck and hid into the back of the pickup truck heading southbound. Their mom had told them that they could not go to the field with their dad. The older son who was with his father sat in the front of the pickup truck. As the two vehicles approached the intersection, there was a terrible collision. The driver of the semi appeared to have had a massive heart attack. His foot slammed down on the accelerator causing the truck to lurch into the air, collide with the pickup truck and fly into a huge tree. It all happened so quickly. People who heard it thought it was an airplane crashing into a building. My brother, who was supposed to buy my ticket, was asleep in the back with a couple of other guys when it took place. When those two trucks collided in midair, they both hit a giant tree, pulling it up from the root. Five people lost their lives that day. My brother and brother-in-law who were on the back of that pickup were both thrown into the air. My brother-in-law landed on the pavement of the highway, my brother landed in the grass across the highway.

The 18-wheeler had pinned the truck against the tree halfway to the top. The four people that were in the cab of the pick-up truck were crushed into the huge tree and unrecognizable. It was one of the most horrible sights I ever witnessed as a young teenager. One of Simon's older sons, my classmate in high school was so injured, the doctor said it would take a miracle to save him since over 80 of his bones were broken in his body. His body was like a jellyfish because nothing was attached. *Oh, God!*

But, when the saints prayed and the mothers travailed, they brought forth healing and deliverance I had not seen in a long time. Simon's two younger sons died in the crash instantly. Their small bodies could not handle the impact of that 18-wheeler. An older guy with the young man driving the 18-wheeler died at the scene. The driver of the 18-wheeler was badly hurt, but did not die. As a result of the crash, the tree landed on the roof of the building outside the store entrance where there were two benches. People would sit there to eat their lunches and great conversations would take place there. Well, on that day it would become a memorial. One of the highway workers who was sitting there eating his lunch when the tree fell on the roof and part of a limb from the tree fell on him, broke his neck instantly. The father driving the pickup truck, Simon, was killed instantly also. This made a total of five people who lost their lives that day.

Lenny and his wife, Ms. FeFe (all we ever knew or called her) are now deceased. They had owned the store for over 50 years or more. They were inside the door and it shook them to the core. They people in the little small square banded together, picked up the wounded, and took them to the hospital in their cars. If they had called and waited for the ambulance, no one would have made it since it was coming from so far away. To this day, the ambulance service is still over fifty miles away.

I tell you, God came through that little town and removed the dark cloud. Yes, He did! I was so sure that I wouldn't be able to go to Milwaukee for the summer because I had to become the caretaker for my injured brother. I kept praying and made it my business to be the best nurse for my brother as he recovered.

Within a couple weeks, my brother began to feel better and I was able to continue braiding little kids' hair and babysitting to make extra money for my trip. One day, I went into my brother's bedroom to see if he needed anything. I told him that I was short of money to buy my bus ticket for my trip to Milwaukee and my sister-in-law was going to be very disappointed if I didn't go. My brother looked at me and asked, "Do you really wanna go?" He said, "I'm much better now. I have some money I can help you out."

I was like, "Really?"

"Yes," he said.

Well, I got a one-way ticket to Milwaukee. Remember, I had lied that my sister-in-law was going to buy my return ticket before school starts? Nervously, I boarded the bus for Milwaukee, Wisconsin planning heading to an address my sister-in-law no longer lived at.

Thank God I made it to Milwaukee Wisconsin early that morning. I called the phone number I had even though I knew that it was disconnected. There I was in a strange place at a bus station crowded with people. Looking around, I could see people just going about their business. Some were arriving and greeting others. I guessed they may have been returning from a trip, coming for a vacation, or for a funeral. I saw people sitting and waiting for someone to pick them up. I saw people calling cabs, but I had no knowledge of doing any of that for myself. I sat around for most of the day. 10 o'clock turned to 11am and 11 passed to 12 o'clock noon. I just sat there wondering to myself. *What am I going to do because I cannot stay in this bus depot all night. I certainly can't go home now because I only have six dollars left in my pocket.*

I ate the sandwich that I hadn't eaten the night before. I ended up going to the vending machine and buying three moon pies. I loved moon pies!

As I was sitting there trying to figure a way out of my predicament, I noticed a tall slender man watching me. He had on a white three-piece suit, red shoes, red shirt with a red tie, and a red hat with a feather in it. The man kept walking through the bus depot. I noticed that he wouldn't talk to everybody but he would go and talk to lonely girls sitting by themselves. After he talked with them, they would get up and follow him outside. I don't know what happened outside but I know that they followed him out but they never came back in with him.

After an hour or so had gone past, I thought I would get up and look outside at the front door of the bus depot. By the time I got up and made it to the door, this tall man who was about six feet tall had an unusual grin on his face. He stopped me as though he knew me. He was trying to hold a conversation with me but I remember my mother's voice telling me not to talk to strangers. "Don't say nothing to them and don't go nowhere with them. You stay right there at that bus depot and call your sister so she can come and get you."

The tall man approached me and said, "You know I've been waiting to pick up this young lady. She's a friend of my mother's but she has not come yet. I have waited on three different buses and she's not been on any of those buses. When I saw some young ladies that I knew, I took them home and then I came back up here." Then he said, "I'm tired now I'm going to get ready and I'm going to go home for the evening. Maybe they can call me when they arrive."

Then he looked at me with concern. "So who's going to be picking you up? You have been here for a long time."

I didn't want to talk to him but he seemed so nice and his voice was so pleasant. I thought he was a good person. I began to tell him my story. "Well, I came up here to see my sister-in-law and I'm waiting for her to come and pick me up when she gets off work.

"Where does she live?" he asked.

"Here in Milwaukee."

" What's the address?" he wanted to know.

"Well, I just got this address here on a piece of paper." I showed him an old envelope with the old address on it.

And when I did, he said, "I know just where that is."

"You do?" I couldn't believe it.

"Yeah, that's not too far from where I'm going. I took the other young ladies over there in that area. It's getting late. I can drop you off if you want me to or you can call your family and let them know that I'll be bringing you home."

Now, I began to think. *Well, maybe he's not so bad you know. I'm like, I can't stay here in this bus stop all night. I'm getting worried and he is the friendliest person that I have talked to since I made it to Milwaukee.*

"You got some luggage?" he asked, anxious to help.

"Yeah." I hesitated, not so excited to go with him.

"So you sure you don't want to go?"

"That's okay," I insisted.

"Okay," he responded. He turned as if to leave and then all of a sudden, he acted as if he had forgotten to get something. He walked over to the vending machine and bought two pops. Turning to me, he asked, "What's your favorite?"

"Root beer."

So he bought me a root beer. "Thank you," I said. That root beer was nice and cold. And because I was thirsty, it was just what I needed.

"You're welcome," he replied before heading towards the door again. "You sure you don't want me to drop you off? I don't want to leave you here in this bus depot all night by yourself. You know it could be very dangerous for you, you know. "He went on, "I just want to make sure that you get to where you're going safe."

My heart melted and I finally said "Okay." Deep down inside of me something kept saying, *Don't do it!*

But fear of being stuck at the bus depot gripped my heart. Besides, I didn't know what was going to happen to me as I had less than $6 in my pocket. So I grabbed my suitcase. He reached over to take it from my hand.

"I'll carry it," he offered.

"I got it," I said.

"Okay, come on. My car is right down here."

When I looked out the door, I saw this cab. His car was parked just ahead of the cab.

I stood looking at the cab sitting outside right in front of the door. A lady stepped out. She was a big woman and stood around 6 feet tall! If I had to describe her, I would say that she looked well built like an Amazon woman. When I saw her, I desperately wanted to speak to her but as I started to open my mouth, he stopped me.

"Come on and don't worry. She is going to charge you too much money and remember you have less than $6 in your pocket."

But I had never said how much money I had in my pocket. Now mind you, none of this is making sense to me until years later. I didn't think about it then but he reminded me that since I had less than $6 in my pocket, the cab was going to charge me more money than I would be able to pay. He wanted me to believe that I could go with him and it would be free. He would drop me off at my home and I would be safe with my sister-in-law.

Deep in my heart, I knew even if he dropped me off there, she didn't live there anymore. Still, I really wanted to find her because I was so desperate to have

an experience in a different environment than I had
grown up in all my life.

He tried to rush me past the taxi lady. I thought
I could at least ask her how much the fare would be.
She looked at him and he looked at her. She didn't ask
me any questions or anything but she opened the back
door and said, "Get in this car now!"

I looked at her. I realized that even though I did
not know this lady, I was not afraid. At the same time,
I wasn't offended because she spoke with authority
like my mother used to when she would give me a direct command. I had learned to distinguish when my
mom was playing or not so serious from when she
wanted me to do something urgently.

She repeated, "Get in this car right now, young
lady. I'm taking you to where your family is."

It did not worry me or frighten me because I believed she was taking me to my family. I quickly
obeyed because of the authority of her voice. I had my
luggage and I jumped into the back of the car.

I noticed the tall man never came close to the
car. He stayed his distance but his language became
vile and nasty. She yelled at him, "Get away from her.
You cannot have her!"

She got in, closed the door, and we drove off.
Mind you, I never said a word because I was terrified.
As we drove away, I looked back through the window
and saw that tall man in the white suit, with red shoes,
red shirt, and a stripe or a white stripe tie, jumping up
and down, pointing his finger, and swearing at her and
the car. I stared at him. I sensed something evil that I
didn't even fully understand at the time. Here was the

devil trying to get me by using this man to lure me into a trap. But God had protected me from harm.

The cab driver looked back at me from her mirror and said, "Young lady where do you think you're going now?"

My heart was really beating fast. I couldn't call my mother. I didn't know where I was and I didn't have my sister-in- law's correct number or address. I was at the mercy of God. I quickly made up a lie. I told her I came here looking for my sister-in-law because we had a death in the family and my mother wanted me to find her. I knew that was so lame.

She looked at me again. "Tell me, lady, where are you going?"

Something about the way she said it gripped my heart. I knew I had better tell her the truth. I sensed if I told her the truth I would be alright. Don't get me wrong now. I was not thinking spiritually. I was just thinking intellectually because I'm a smart girl. At least I thought I was.

"He preys on young ladies. He takes them to a place and makes them prostitutes, selling their bodies."

My heart began to melt and the words tumbled out as I told her the whole story of how I was born and raised in Mississippi. I told her that my family was very poor and I didn't have any money. I admitted that I lied to my parents and told them I had my sister-in-law's phone number and her address and how I con-

vinced my brother to help me buy my one way bus
ticket. Now, if I didn't find my sister-in-law, I
wouldn't have a way to get home.

She looked at me and asked, "Do you know
who that man was back there at the bus station?" She
went on to enlighten me. "He preys on young ladies.
He takes them to a place and makes them prostitutes,
selling their bodies. He gets them hooked on drugs and
puts them out on the streets. Soon they will do anything for those drugs, carrying their dope from one end
of the city to the next. When they're done with you,
nobody will want you. Then they do away with you.
They may kill you or just leave you on the street where
you might die from any manner of disease."

I began to weep. Then she said, "Wipe your
face. You are going to be all right, but I don't ever want
to see you do this again. You have a bright future ahead
of you. In your future you are going to open doors for a
lot of people. You will help a lot of people and mend a
lot of people because you're not afraid and you dare to
be different."

Then she told me she had to go back to work
since she was not off her shift yet. She had the day shift
and had to work until the night shift came on. In the
meantime, she offered to take me to her home. I could
stay there until she returned.

I should have been afraid but I was not. She
pulled up to this big beautiful house with a driveway
on the side. I could hear the sound of kids in the backyard, but because of the closed gate, I could not see
them. She got out of the cab. I could see she had put on
a hat like a policeman and one long black braid was
hanging down her back. Her feet looked real big to me

as I followed her into the house. There, she introduced me to a boy and a girl.

"I want you guys to stay here and play." Then motioning towards me she said, "This is Dollie. I want you guys to take care of her until I return. Then I'm going to make your favorite dish."

I had never told her my name nor do I remember telling her that my favorite dish at that time was spaghetti and meatballs. It is still one of my favorites. I was so happy and I felt safe. She gave us permission to have some ice cream and cookies. We always were allowed to make some Kool-Aid and play in the backyard. She would be back in a few hours.

I don't know what time she came back but when she did, we were all so happy to see her. She told me her name was Evelyn. I really felt good then because my sister at home was Evelyn too.

She went in the kitchen and in what seemed like 5 or 10 minutes we were sitting at the table eating spaghetti and meatballs. When we finished, my newfound friends wanted me to stay. I still didn't even know all their names but I think one of the guys was named Raymond. I can't remember the other young ladies names either but they really didn't want me to leave. She told them I had to go and be with my family. They all were asking, "When are you going to come back and see us?"

"When I am with my sister, she'll bring me back over here," I told them.

So my angel (that's how I refer to her now) said, "Come on let's go find your family." We got into the car and I gave her the old address I had that was on the envelope. I also gave her the old phone number which was disconnected even before I left Mississippi.

When we got to the address, some other people were living there. I stayed in the car as she went up and she talked to them. From what I could see, she was doing most of the talking. I just watched hoping that she could find my sister-in-law. A few minutes later, she came back and began driving up one hill and down. We went around the corner near the freeway and I wondered where we were headed. *Were we ever going to find my family?*

Just then, we pulled up in front of a house. She told me to take my suitcase and go ring the doorbell. She also gave me a piece of paper with her address on it.

"Maybe your sister-in-law can bring you by to play with Raymond and the others before you have to go back home to Mississippi." she said.

"Okay," I said. But now I'm trying to figure out how she knew this was my sister-in-law house. *Is she going to leave me here?*

At her word, I went up on the porch and rang the doorbell. Imagine my delight to see one of my younger nephews come to the door. He didn't know me but I knew who he was. I was older than him and we played together before they moved away years ago.

I said, "I am your Auntie Dollie."

He looked confused and he replied, "I don't know who Dollie is." By this time, my sister-in-law asked, "Who are you talking to?

By this time, my sister-in-law asked, "Who are you talking to? Please do not play at the door."

"Somebody is at the door saying she's my auntie."

My sister-in-law just screamed in amazement. "Who are you with and how did you get here?" She thought my mother or my brother or somebody else was with me.

I told her I was here by myself.

"What are you doing up here?" She looked puzzled.

I told her I came because I wanted to get away for the summer. I had saved my money and purchased a bus ticket.

After all the excitement and commotion, I finally looked around and saw that the car was gone.

She asked, "Did you pay the driver?"

"No," I murmured. I didn't have any money to pay her.

"I can't believe this," she said. "I have got to get word to your mom and let her know that you are here safely. I can't believe you found me. I just moved over here a couple months ago. There's no way anybody down there even knew I had moved. I really hadn't told anyone I had moved because I was trying to get away from my crazy husband."

That crazy husband was my brother. Their complicated relationship was a whole story all by itself. I showed her the old address that I had and told her I had only bought a one-way ticket. I told her everything. I knew I had to come clean and tell her the truth from the beginning.

"Wow!" was all she could say. Then she added, "I am so glad to see somebody from down there. I can't believe that you would still want to come and see me."

"I love you," I said. Although she was much older than me, I used to love to spend the night at her house. My nephews were all so excited to see me. They began asking me questions about their grandmother and their other cousins who they had lost touch with.

I was happy to tell them about everybody. I told them how everybody talks about them and how my grandmother loves them so very much. We giggled, we laughed. We ate hot dogs, cookies, and ice cream.

My sister-in-law finally said, "I'm going to bed." But the rest of us talked all night long and we really got to know each other. After a week had gone by, I told my sister that I could only stay for another week. I had to go home.

She agreed and planned to buy my return ticket home. I had promised Evelyn that I would stop by and see her sometime. I really wanted to go over and thank her for being so nice to me.

My sister-in-law was going to have Wednesday off and so we made plans to go that day. She also promised to take me shopping to get some summer stuff and school clothes so I'd have a fresh wardrobe when I returned home. I couldn't wait for Wednesday to arrive.

As I come to the end of this story, my question to you is, do you believe in angels? There certainly are good angels and bad angels. I certainly thank God for my guardian angel.

When Wednesday came, my sister-in-law did as she promised. We drove over to the address Evelyn had given me. To our surprise, we arrived at an empty parking lot. There was no house and no backyard. The only thing there was the driveway.

"Are you sure this is the right place?" my sister-in-law looked confused.

"This is the address she gave me." We drove around the neighborhood looking for the house. I could not find the house or recognize the area, so we went home puzzled.

"I know you didn't write this address because you don't know anything about Milwaukee," she comforted me.

Then I told her what happened at the bus depot and she immediately began to cry. "Oh my God!" she said. "Honey, don't ever do this again. You can come see me anytime you're ready but make sure that you talk to me first. Write to me because you could have been picked up by one of those pimps, those evil men. They have women that work the streets and the bus depot, the train depot, the airport. They are always looking for runaways and strays. They're so familiar with the territory that they know who is new and they know who is lost and who is not. Please don't ever do that again!"

She was emotional and grateful. "You know it was by the grace of God that He kept you, right? Do you believe in angels?"

I had to say, "yes, I do." I realized that I had had an encounter with my guardian angel who covered and protected me that day at the bus depot. My angel was there to protect and fight for me. My encounter with that man in the white suit could have gone so differently. My life could have been devastated and destroyed that day but God protected me. Thank God that He had a plan for my life. I thank God for my encounter with my guardian angel.

GOD not only protected me that summer but He gave me a special memory I could share with my classmates. While I ended up having a fantastic summer with family in Milwaukee, I also know firsthand how God delivered me from a deadly experience with a real life devil disguised as a pimp. The devil was a wolf in sheep's clothing but my ministering angel protected me from his evil attack.

What Happens When God Says, "Let There Be...!"

CHAPTER 2

God Said, "Be Filled With The Spirit"
"He filled me with the Holy Ghost"

"And be not drunk with wine, wherein is excess; but be filled with the Spirit."
-Ephesians 5:18

The book of Ephesians is believed to be one of the most profound works in the entire Bible. This book gives us the perfect picture of God's redemptive pur-pose for our lives from the very beginning. His plan for us was already created before we were manifested or created in Genesis. Ephesians shows us that we were chosen in Christ Jesus by faith before the foundation of the world. Elohim (the Godhead) knew that we would need to be filled with His Spirit in order for everything He had done or spoken concerning us in the beginning is brought into our remembrance.

We were downloaded from heaven into our designated parents whether they are young or older. We already had the language of heaven embedded in our DNA because we came from God. Before sin en-tered into the Garden of Eden, Adam spoke God's lan-guage. He knew how to communicate with God.

Notice, he talked with God. But after sin entered, he hid from God.

The Holy Spirit was there in the beginning, He is one of the Godhead (Trinity) who was there to do his part in creation. Now the Holy Spirit teaches us the language of heaven and He gives us the interpretations. He makes intercession for us when we don't even know what or how to pray to God. I am so glad that the Lord filled me with the Holy Spirit when I was a young girl growing up in Tchula, Mississippi in June, 1973.

Growing up in Mississippi. I was a very outspoken person. I was so outspoken that the elderly thought of me as a very misbehaved young lady. In my time, they called you "fast." Today, it is promiscuous. I was never disrespectful the way they thought. My crime was that I was being educated and I could see more than just a bird's eye view on life. I began to see with the vision of an eagle. I read books and magazines that took me to other places in the world. With my vivid imagination, I went everywhere through the books I read. I was learning that the world I had been living in was only a dot in the world that God had created. I had been sheltered far too long.

So, leading up to the week before I got baptized, I knew I had all the odds against me. Let me explain. When you got to be a certain age you were asked if you wanted to give your life to God and be baptized. Well, when it came time to ask me, the mothers of the church were slow. So I went up and asked them if I could be on the mourning bench. What's a mourning bench? I am glad you asked. The mourning bench was just another name for the place you sat while *tarrying for the Holy Spirit.*

The mourning bench period would last for at least two weeks. Before leading up to your first day on the mourning bench, you have the right to go to one of the mothers and ask her to be your intercessor, mentor, prayer partner or what you might need them to be. They would then accept your invitation. Well, I was the last one in and I got the meanest mother on the motherboard. I remember that she and my mother did not see eye to eye on a whole lot of things. Yeah, they did their best to hide their disagreements but sometimes my mother would set her straight. My friends and I saw from their body language how they cut their eyes at each other.

Anyhow, I ended up with her as my mentor. During this period of *tarrying,* you could not go outside to play, watch television, or listen to the radio. The only exception for the radio was listening to gospel music. You had to fast for some hours of the day and pray. Assigned chores were very light duty since they wanted you to stay focused. They would even go as far as to instruct you to ask the Lord to show you a sign that you have religion.

Well, I was a student of the word of God. My daddy studied the Bible all the time and he would often teach me the word of God. So, I had a different way of talking to the Lord. I knew how to read His word and although did not have a clear understanding of the whole thing, I learned how to cry out to God. In my heart I truly wanted a relationship with the Lord. I must admit it started out as me thinking about the new clothes, shoes your parents would buy for the baptism-- a new white sheet, white socks, and a white scarf for your hair with a plastic bag to keep your hair from getting wet.

Let me explain. Back in those days, when a child on the mourning bench got filled with the Holy Ghost, they would get all brand new clothes and shoes for their baptism. It was like a wedding day or prom but with glorified clothes. You were born again with a new walk, new talk, and new attitude. But around the second day on the mourning bench, my appetite changed. I no longer wanted those things, I just wanted what my daddy talked about, having an experience or encounter with God.

Can you believe that some of the kids on the mourning bench with me prayed and asked God to show them a sign? For example, show me 5 black birds. Well, Mississippi is full of black birds. Or another might pray, give me a burning in my heart. I was thinking you are asking for heartburn? Trust me, I am not making light of their experiences. All I know is that this was not enough for me. I needed more.

Each night was a revival night and different preachers would come and preach. I found it strange that none of the messages were teaching about baptism or a relationship with God. So I began to talk to the Lord for myself. I said:

"So God, when you fill me with the Holy Ghost then maybe the Holy Ghost will help me to do it right."

"Lord, I know that you are mighty and that you hold the sky, the moon, the sun and the stars in Your hands. My daddy has told me that the Earth is Your footstool. And from that perspective, I see you as a giant! So God, if my daddy says that You are that big and You are that great, Lord I want to know You, the God my daddy knows. My daddy told me that You were His Daddy and now I want You to be my Daddy, too. God, I want You to do something in me that's incredible and life changing to make my mommy and my daddy proud. God, I know that I have not always been good but I have not always been bad either. I want to go to Sunday school. I want to wear new shoes, I want to wear a new dress and I want my hair done pretty with ribbons. I want to be able to help my mommy and my daddy because I see their struggles and I know that they want the best for us. God, if you fill me with the Holy Ghost, I will be filled with Your power and maybe I can help them. God, maybe I can help the man down the street that only has one eye and no legs. I no longer want to be afraid of him but help me be his friend. My father told me that the gift of the Holy Ghost is free. It is called salvation. Salvation is free, a gift you gave to us. All I have to do is ask for forgiveness for my sins and you will give me salvation. God, I know that those mothers and some of the Deacons don't seem to like me because they say I talk too much and that I'm a fast little girl. But God, sometimes I get confused when I go to church and when I go to school. When I'm in school they teach me to say "yes and no, thank you, may I, not you may not." They teach me to speak what's on my heart and what's on my mind. But then when I go to church and say yes and no, they feel like I have disrespected them. The school teaching is difficult for me but I want to embrace it so that I can get good grades. So God, when you fill me with the Holy Ghost then maybe the Holy Ghost will help me to do it right. And God if you fill me with the Holy Ghost, I will be good to my friend because my daddy said that you will walk beside me everywhere I go and You'll teach me what to say and when to say it the right way. God, if you fill me with the Holy Ghost I want to preach your word. I want to tell everybody about your free gift of the Holy Ghost. God, I hope it's not a bad thing but I don't always want to stay here on this plantation. I want to go out and I want to see the world because I see all that You have made in the books I read in school. God, when I'm looking into my books I can see in my mind how the Earth is your footstool. And God, everywhere you place your feet is where I want to go. If I have the Holy Ghost then I will believe that will be possible. So God, I want you to be my friend and I want the Holy Ghost to be my friend. I want to thank you because you died for my sins. So God I want you to be my very special friend and I want to have a relationship with you like you have with my daddy. And God, I want to be baptized in the water and I want to be filled with the Holy Ghost."

And God honored this little girls' prayer. In the very place where I was talking to the Lord, I felt a heat come over my body. I felt something on the inside of me that made me feel like a balloon full of energy, strength, and love. I felt so full, I thought I would burst. I ran to my mother crying. I told her my stomach was hurting and my chest was hurting. She felt my head and my stomach. My head wasn't hot and my stomach wasn't cold so she said, "You don't have a fever and your stomach is not cold." In those days if your stomach was cold then your stomach was hurting.

"Do you need to go to the bathroom?" she asked.

"No." I told her I was praying and asking God to do something for me when all of a sudden everything started hurting. Not a bad hurt but just something inside of me.

My mother smiled and said, "Thank you, Jesus!" Then she told me to go lay down and get you some rest. That was on August 10, 1967, a Thursday. That was the day that I gave the Lord my heart. And, that night when the service got started, I don't know what type of look was on my face, but I sat there listening to Reverend Edwards preach the word of God and I understood what he was saying from a different perspective. I remember tears rolling down my cheeks and I began to say." Thank you, Jesus. Thank you, Lord." And that same feeling I felt earlier that day happened again.

My feelings towards my intercessor who I thought was the meanest woman in the church changed. I did not feel that way toward her anymore. She moved up, got her handkerchief, and gave it to me. She wiped my tears and told me, "You got it!"

The pastor, in the middle of his sermon, looked at her with a smile. With a big grin, she nodded her head. I will never ever forget that night nor the experience I had with God. When the appeal of the altar call came, I was still hesitant because I wasn't exactly sure what was going to take place. I looked at the pastor. He looked at the woman I thought was the meanest mother. Then my eyes were opened. She wasn't the meanest mother, she was a woman sold out to God and she was not going to be about any foolishness.

She came up and asked me about my experience with the Lord. I just broke down and cried. I told her that I wanted God to be my Father, my friend and my saviour. I told her that I promised God that I would preach his Word to all who would listen. Then I went up and sat in the seat of the righteous because I was no longer a sinner without hope. Now I was a sinner who had been pardoned and given the gift of salvation. What began as my way to get new clothes, new shoes, and new hairdos turned into the beginning of a new relationship with the Lord that weekend.

I learned that when you receive God into your life everything becomes new. A new mindset. Your attitude is no longer the same, your thoughts are no longer the same. The way you talk is no longer the same. You lose the desire to go to those forbidden places and do the forbidden things. Now don't get me wrong. That doesn't mean that I didn't make mistakes over and over again. I was learning to trust my new friend but sometimes as a child I was just immature. I did not always understand His ways. Isaiah 55:9 reminds us that "His ways are not our ways."

But thank God that He did not give up on me. I will not give up on you either! I was still on The Potter's Wheel and God was transforming my life everyday. That week, my mother went shopping and she bought me a brand new dress. The dress had 3/4 quarter length sleeves like a bell with laces of gold around them. The color of the dress was woven with different colors ivory, brown, beige, sparkles of gold dust blended in. It was so pretty. My shoes were gold with the toe slightly pointed up, almost like the shoes of Aladdin. That was the first time that I wore stockings and they were off-white to blend in with my dress. My sister had done my hair in a french roll with spiral curls in the front and my mother had brought me a beautiful pin to put in my french roll hairdo. Oh! It was going to be a grand day. I couldn't hardly sleep that night.

On August 12, 1967, the sun rose at 5:58 am. At 9:am we were ready for the service. I was so nervous because we knew that everybody would be there for the baptism. In those days when we got baptized, there were no baptismal pools in the church. We got baptized in a lake called Bee Lake. Let me describe this lake to you.

Bee Lake is about a 1400 acre oxbow lake, a curved lake formed where the main stream of the river has cut across the narrow end and no longer flows around the loop of the bend. It was not just a lake but a natural life source for most of the people who lived near it and people came from far and near to draw its water. In Holmes County, it is one of the largest natural lakes. It runs along the bluff line to the flatlands of the Delta and the forest uplands of Yazoo, Mississippi. This lake was formed by the southern span of the Ohio River. Interestingly, it was this same Ohio River which served as a route to freedom for fugitive slaves going North.

Escaping slaves looked forward to arriving in Ripley, Ohio and climbing the famous '*Freedom Stairway*,' the 100 steps leading up to the John Rankin House. John Rankin (1793-1886) was a Presbyterian minister and educator who devoted most of his life to the antislavery movement. His house was a station on the Underground Railroad and the stairs up to his house was a beacon of hope for slaves. The stairs became a door to freedom at the end of a perilous journey and slaves rejoiced at the welcome they found at the top of the hill.

Now back to Bee Lake. It was so significant in our community and a life source for the people in surrounding areas. The lake was a place of gatherings and brought people together-- Black, White, Hispanic, Chinese, Indians because of its resources.

"Glory To God!" I started shouting, dancing and speaking in a language unknown to me."

Bee Lake also provided food for many families. People traveled up and down the lake placing their nets in the water and catching fish. On land, many trapped animals like beaver, minks, raccoon, rabbits and deer. Some animals were used for food and others were sold for their furs. Firewood was also gathered along the lake.

The lake provided a place of escape when you needed to get away from everybody and just have a little peace and be quiet. Sometimes the lake would be so still and peaceful. The only sounds you heard were those of frogs croaking, birds chipping, fish sucking on the tree fungus and the deers panting for its cool water.

But there were also times when Bee Lake would take lives. The most dangerous times were when the lake overflowed from the heavy downpours of rain. Our house sat up on a hill near the lake. When the lake overflowed, dangerous predators like alligators, and snakes lurking in the water would come right into our backyard. Sometimes people would die in the lake or along its banks.

Most importantly, Bee Lake served as a place of spiritual freedom for people who went down into the water to identify with Jesus. Over the years, Christians in that community hollowed out a special place along the riverbank where they used it only for baptisms. On the morning of baptisms, the deacons of the church would go down to the riverbank where they had cut out trees, cut the grass and put wooden planks, and layers of tin so our feet would not be dirty or muddy.

On that particular Saturday morning, the day of my baptism, August 12, 1967, we all met down at the hollowed out landing as it was called. Gloria Jean Mason, Thomas Allen Trent (now deceased), and Susie Jean Smith (also deceased) were the candidates for baptism. I don't remember the exact person who was baptized first or second. I remember them coming out shivering cold. The mothers would have a sheet ready to wrap up in and lead us up the hill.

All I know is that when it was my turn to go into the water, the pastor and the deacon led me down in the water. I was so ready. They held my nose and told me to cross my hands over my chest as though I was being laid in a casket. They laid me backward in the water and the water covered my whole face and body. It seemed like I was suspended in the water for a few minutes. I could clearly see the sun and the glow of rays shining down on me. Then they brought me up!!!!

"Glory To God!" I started shouting, dancing and speaking in a language unknown to me. I was sooo very hot. I didn't know it was the Holy Ghost all over me. The mothers tried to put a sheet around me but I didn't want a sheet on me. They were still trying to tie me down until my mother encouraged them to let me go. I praised God until everybody on the bank was praising the Lord.!!! I went down as a sinner but I came up a free child in the LORD!

On that day, Bee Lake served as a vehicle to carry me to spiritual freedom. My filthy sins were washed away in this flowing stream. Wow!!! What a great day that was! August is the eight month on the calendar and it represents a new beginning. The tenth of August is the day I gave my hand to the LORD. Ten represents cycles of completeness. It is connected to a perfect period of waiting. Twelve, the number of authority and perfection, represents the church, faith, and is a symbol of perfect government of God. Thirteen is associated with suffering. "But, Jesus said if you suffer with me you shall reign with me. (2 Timothy 2:12). It was time to do spiritual warfare with the devil and his imps.

But, I still had a lot to learn. That Sunday morning after my baptism, something different had happened to me. Now when I went to Sunday School I didn't go to terrorize my cousin who was our Sunday school teacher and the church administrator. Normally, I went to church because I loved listening to good singing and the preacher preaching the word of God. Although I was not living for the Lord, I was drawn to it. I believe it was because the way my father would tell me all the stories of the Bible. He would make the stories come alive. My daddy would explain the word to me, breaking it down and giving me everyday examples of what it means and how to apply it to my life. Well, sometimes I misused my knowledge. I tried to intimidate my Sunday School teacher. She was a very dedicated teacher, the kind of teacher who bought the kids treats, especially those who came on time, studied, and participated in class activities. I came late all the time just to bug her and I had the nerve to expect a treat most of the time. Although I got treats, I knew that she must have hated it when I would come through the church doors. She knew that trouble had just come through the doors.

For example, while she was teaching I would always raise my hand to ask her awkward questions that I knew she did not have answers for. Even before she could answer the question, I would be preparing a rebuttal or another question. She would threaten to tell my parents but that didn't stop me. I was a bold little girl. I would sit there with this smirky smile on my face not saying anything but sending the message, "Yep, I said it, now what?"

Remember, I was the kind of person that did not have a problem in speaking my mind. Whatever came to my mind, I would let you have it. I just didn't have any control over my tongue but I really was a compassionate person. The Holy Ghost is the only one who can bridle the tongue and I was missing the indwelling of the Holy Spirit. But, the day the Lord filled me with the Holy Ghost down by the river, my life changed forever. I came to respect and lend a helping hand to my cousin, the teacher I used to terrorize in Sunday School.

Years later, still serving as a Sunday School teacher and church administrator, she invited me to preach at the church's 90th anniversary celebration. Oh God! What an honor that was for me and her. God gave her an opportunity to see that the fruit of her labor was not in vain. Because of her faithfulness to Sunday School and service as church administrator, she was able to provide me with the exact dates of my baptism and when I joined church for me to include in this book. The records were still there. Some may think well that is what administrators are supposed to do. But can you imagine that those records were written in pencil over 50 years ago? Computers, xerox machines were not handed to a small church and town like ours. Thank God that those records were still readable. To Jesus be the Glory! The Holy Ghost preserved what was important to me, my past present and future. And He will preserve you!

CHAPTER 3

Bittersweet

Writing this chapter is a bit challenging. Actually, it is bittersweet for me. In this chapter I share how I learned to obey God rather than man. In this chapter my flesh was crucified by the church leaders whom I loved and trusted. I thought I was going to die. I had shortness of breath and oh, the shame. But, what the enemy meant for evil, God used for my good. He had already spoken his promise in Jeremiah 29:11 over my life: "For I know the plans I have for you, declares the Lord, plans to prosper you and not to harm you, plans to give you hope and a future."

What I thought was killing me was only stripping me, emptying me, and positioning me for greatness! I could praise God like Peter did: "Praise be to the God and Father of our Lord Jesus Christ! In his great mercy he has given us new birth into a living hope through the resurrection of Jesus Christ from the dead." (I Peter 1:3 NIV)

I discovered the promise of new life Paul taught about in 2 Corinthians 5:17: "Therefore if any man be in Christ, he is a new creature: old things are passed away; behold, all things are become new."

This chapter recounts the dawning of a new beginning in my life. The Bible tells us that Jesus Christ

died for our sins; he was wounded for our transgres-
sions and the chastisement of our peace was upon his
shoulders (Isaiah 53:5). The words that were spoken
over my life, whether negative or positive, could not
derail my future. Jesus paid the price for my pain and
suffering. I no longer see myself with the flaws that
man points out. According to the book of Psalms, "I
am fearfully and wonderfully made." (Psalms 139:14).

The result of Adam and Eve's sin in the Garden
of Eden caused God's creation to become distorted.
They shifted humans out of our rightful place and as a
result, all people inherited a distorted, ugly, and sinful
nature. To fashion something beautiful of my life again,
our God, had to put me on *the Potter's Wheel.* I was
marred, but I was in the hands of the potter. God had
his hand upon me and He was reworking me in his
hands, (See Jeremiah 18)

In the previous chapter, I shared about the time
the Lord filled me with the Holy Spirit. Later, I was
hurt by the church but I did not die. Let me tell a bit
more about the extended version of my new beginning.
Although I was raised in the church from birth, I was
not saved nor did I have a relationship with Jesus
Christ. When I got filled with the Holy Ghost, my
whole life shifted. My eyes were opened and like Isaiah, the old prophet, who spoke saying "I beheld the
Lord high and lifted up and his train filled the temple."
(Isaiah 6:1-6) That is when my life changed forever. I
did not see exactly what Isaiah saw, but I saw the Lord
and I felt His love pouring into me. I knew that for the
rest of my life I would be committed to Him and His
work.

I think back on how I came to Chicago. When I arrived, I lived near my cousin. Before living in Chicago, I was not used to going to church every Sunday. Our church service was powerful when we came together on the second Sunday of each month. Another church service would be held on the first Sunday, third Sunday and so forth. Each Sunday, a different church had their service. A lot of it was based on tradition but when I went to church, I felt connected to my family.

But down through the years, I learned why the Lord has brought me to Chicago. In Isaiah 55: 8-11, we read that "the Lord's ways are not our ways and his thoughts are not our thoughts." Based on my thoughts and my ways, I believed that I was leaving home to make a new life for me and my son and to get away from the country. While that was true, God always had a different plan for my life. I am so glad He did.

While living with my cousin, we started going to a little church on the southside of Chicago called Holy Ghost Fire Baptist Pentecostal Church. Our great leader, mentor, father figure there was the late Pastor Reverend Leroy Johnson, a mechanic by trade. I attended that church for 18 years. My pastor taught me everything I needed to know about how to operate and function fully in a church. It was there that I recommitted my life to the Lord wholeheartedly. In this church I received the baptism of the Spirit and spoke in tongues fluently for the second time. It was where I allowed the Holy Spirit full control of my life.

It all started in my kitchen one week while I was washing dishes. I began to sing the old chorus, *"Walk With Me, Lord"*-- Walk with me Lord, walk with me. While I am on this tedious journey, I need you, Jesus, to walk with me."

Suddenly, it felt like a wind came into my home and I lost myself in the presence of the Lord. When I came to myself, my feet did look new because they were white with the fibers from my carpet. I had danced until I was soaking wet. I had had a Holy Ghost encounter with the Lord. But it did not stop there. Sitting in the pew at church the following Sunday morning, the Holy Spirit overshadowed me again. I began speaking in tongues as the Spirit gave utterance.

"When I began in this ministry, I had not planned on preaching."

After that day, nothing was the same in my life. There were times when I felt out of place among my church family because it seemed the Lord had elevated me to another level of anointing. My language changed, my thoughts changed, and my walk changed. People around me saw the transformation taking place in my life as I was growing spiritually. When they saw my authentic relationship with God, people began coming to me with their issues and their problems. For a while, things were pretty good. My pastor saw the call of God in my life and He ordained me to be an evangelist.

When I began in this ministry, I had not planned on preaching. But God had other plans for me. God knew the call that he had on my life from the beginning and He knew that one day I would preach the gospel. One night while asleep, I began to dream and it appeared like a vision God was showing me. In this dream I was an eagle soaring on wings high up in the sky. The vision from so high into the sky was breath-taking! From one mountain to another, I soared. At each mountain, I was greeted by people-- men, women, and children--who appeared like birds flapping their wings. They were literally jumping up off of the ground, happy to see me. As I moved towards them, I was dropping bits of food into their mouths. But the strangest thing was that my feet never touched the ground. The movement of air caused by the span of my wings was blowing all the debris from around them allowing them to feast upon their meal. Then I would take flight and go to another high mountain. I would repeat the process of delivering food into the mouths of men, women, and children, again and again.

Through this dream, the Lord told me that He would always give me food to feed his people. God confirmed to me through the affirmation of several people that He could trust me with His word. I did not understand all of it then, but I understand more now. The Lord began to use me to preach the gospel. The more I preached, the more I realized that there was more to God than what I was preaching. As my appetite for God's word grew, I knew that I was being limited by where I was.

It was not until after three years of this strong impression from the Lord that I finally left my church. It was if the Lord was saying to me, I need you to go to a place that I'm going to show you. I had been reluctant to go because I was so comfortable where I was. I didn't have to worry about anything. My car would be taken for a car wash by the deacons. They would fill my tank with gas. If my car broke down, my pastor was the first person I would call, even before my husband, because I knew he could fix my car.

But one day, the Lord spoke to me. "Will you die in Egypt?" I rebuked the devil. I could not believe that God would send me from a place of luxury and comfort to a place of rocks and trenches. I did not understand what God was talking about when He told me there was so much work still to be done in that ministry. Yet, God knew that my work there was done and that He needed to send me somewhere else to prepare for my next level.

I began to attend a Bible study that was held everyday. All day long, at the home of two pastors, God began to download into me. The illumination of His Word I received was like nothing I had ever known before. These two people blessed my life, my children, and my ministry. They taught me how to dig into the word of God for myself. The more I dug into his Word, the thirstier I became. I remember the female pastor always saying that the early bird gets the worm. Well, I became an early bird.

I lived in Chicago but I had a job in Arlington Heights where I would have to be at work at 5:30am in the morning. I was so thirsty and hungry for the more of God that I went to unbelievable lengths. Psalms 34:8 challenged me. "Oh taste and see that the Lord is good." When I tell you that God is good, God is so good. The female Pastor would tell us if you want God and if you mean business, meet here at 3 a.m. for one hour of prayer. For some people who worked a 9 to 5 job, or those who had to be at work at 7 or 8 am, that might have been manageable if they lived in the area. As for me, I had to be at work at 5 a.m. in the morning. I had to have all my line workers stocked and filled and ready for their shift at 5:25 a.m.

When your thirst is greater than your circumstances, you will do the extraordinary. God's word is true--"Like the hart (deer) who pants after the water brooks, so panteth my soul after thee, O God." (Psalms 42:1). I would get up every morning at 2:30 am, get dressed, and go all the way to 4700 South King Drive. I would lay out before God crying asking God to show me the way and give me more of Him.

The more I cried out to God, the more He showed me things about myself. The more I asked of Him, the more I had to die to my flesh and materialistic things. I had gotten so accustomed to and comfortable with things that did not satisfy. For example, I loved hanging out with my friends and going on vacation. I was more carnally-minded than spiritually-minded. I was learning that a carnal mind should never reign supreme over our spiritual mind.

God was getting me ready for a journey. My friends and family would not accompany me for a certain period of time. Remember the story of Moses? When he fled Egypt, God caused him to be hidden on the backside of the mountain for a period for forty years. Well, my mountain was not being invited to certain gatherings that I used to attend. Strange conversations started happening about my lifestyle. I had no clue. I didn't realize that what I was asking of God would mean Him removing me from an environment that I had gotten comfortable with. I had to empty myself of things that had kept me stagnant. There were things I had been okay with, things I had I settled with. The more I prayed and asked for more of Him and the clarity of His word, my appetite for spiritual things grew. I kept asking and reaching. And glory to God, my faith was rewarded. God fed me manna from heaven. God took away an environment that was impeding my growth.

As I grew in His Word, the scales began to fall off my eyes. I finally could see things clearly. The Holy Spirit began to remind me of things God had been speaking to me from when I was very young. He showed me a future of traveling, preaching, helping people, and taking care of people. Just as God used David as a shepherd to be one of the greatest of all time, God took the skills He gave me from birth to be able to take care of young babies and channeled that compassion into a ministry of helping, loving, and blessing people.

I am inspired to lead and teach others about who Jesus Christ is and what He did on the cross at Calvary Hill. God taught me patience, temperance, meekness, joy, and faith through the Holy Ghost. Now I understand what God meant when he said that if I stayed in Egypt, I will surely die. I was blinded by darkness in plain daylight by being in a place that was limited. The environment didn't have the requisite spiritual resources or the cutting edge anointing I needed to battle the evil spirits I would one day have to face. I was boxed in and no one recognized the power of God's anointing that was upon my life.

When it was time for me to move on, it was one of the hardest things that I ever had to do. I never thought I would leave the church that had reminded me so much of my hometown. When I left, I did it the right way and I wrote a letter to my pastor, the motherboard, and the Deacon board. I needed them to know that I loved them and that no one had done anything to me. It was just that God was taking me on another journey and I needed to obey the leading of God.

My pastor was not happy with my decision, but we remained on great terms. I often go back and visit the church to share the message of the word. They were some of the pillars in my life and they helped build a stable foundation for my life. But sometimes you just need to be courageous, trust God, and go.

I went on to fellowship with a ministry on the southside of Chicago. When I got there, the ministry was very small with only a handful of members. A small group of us with our children had come over together. At first, it seemed to be working beautifully even though we had to learn the character of a new group of people as well as their way of doing things.

Earlier I had mentioned that my pastor had taught me everything I needed to know about operating and maintaining the flow of the church. After learning all I did, it was time for me to move on to the next training ground. All that the pastor had deposited in my life was just what I needed to lead the women's ministry God was about to birth through me.

After joining the new ministry, the pastor immediately recognized the anointing, gifts, and calling that was on our lives and he ordained several of us as elders at the church. I began to move about in the ministry working diligently and lending a helping hand anywhere I could. Because of the training I had received at my previous church, I was a real go-getter. I believed that nothing was impossible for God to accomplish in me. If I could see it, I believed that I could receive it and achieve it. That's what I went after and that's what I did.

Now I know I had flaws then and I still do. But I also knew that God was still working on me. I was helping, training, and teaching others all that I knew about building a ministry. I was supporting the pastor's vision and adding to the kingdom of God. In the 4 years I was in this ministry, we went through many ups and downs. We went from crisis to crisis. Then we started bickering at each other when things didn't get better. I would soon learn some of the hardest life lessons in ministry. I would be stripped, hurt, and wounded to the point that I thought I would just literally lay down and die. Oh God! It hurt!

But, was it for my good? I didn't know how I was going to face my children. I didn't know how I was going to face the world, I just didn't know what I was going to do. I felt like I had made the biggest mistake of my life. Had I missed God? I felt I had been abandoned by all my family and friends. People were still present in my life but the lonely (spirit) told me I was alone. I felt like someone had literally set me on the street and just walked away and left me there. I didn't know where God was. All I know is that I could not stop trusting Him because of how much He loved me.

Through all the early rising and fellowshipping with Him, I had developed a strong trusting relationship with my God. I remembered how He had kept me through the years when I was sick. I recalled how He had healed my daughter who was born with a horse-shoe kidney but was now living a healthy, productive life as the mother of my beautiful granddaughter. I remembered how He protected my son from the streets and gangs of Chicago, Illinois. I could go on and on but I'll just say that I held onto the testimonies in my life and I kept them close to my heart. I refused to grow bitter because I knew that God could not dwell in my heart with bitterness.

Things got so bad I couldn't even talk to the people that I had gone over to the ministry with. It seemed as though they had turned their backs on me. That was another dagger that was in my heart. By the time I had settled into this new ministry, my faith, trust, and love for God was stronger than any hatred, bitterness, or lie that could have been told about me. I went through some things. I will not share them all but I will share that when God is for you, He is more than the world that is against you. "Greater is he that is in me than he that is in the world." (1st John 4:4).

I remember telling a young woman at the ministry once that when I'm not at home that I do not allow young ladies or young men in my home. I needed to be there to be sure that they were safe and supervised. Our children are our greatest investment. I was not going to give place to the devil. So, one day I left home to run some errands and this young lady ended up coming to my house anyway. While I was out, she and my daughter had some words. They were not pleasant words. It got so bad, my nephew ended up calling me. He told me what was going on and that I needed to return home right away.

I wondered what could be happening. He said, "there's about to be a fight in the front of the house."

"Fight with who?" I had no idea.

When he told me the situation, I turned my car around and came home as fast as I could. When I got out of the car, the argument was still going on. I stepped in between the two young ladies, my daughter and our uninvited guest.

"Okay, you guys can you both cool it down! What's going on??" I waited to hear their responses. I waited for our uninvited guest to speak first.

"Your daughter called me a name." she protested.

So I looked at my daughter and asked, "Did you call her a name?"

My daughter bluntly said, "Yes."

I called the blank word and I looked at my daughter. "Did you call her that?"

"Yes, that's how she was acting."

I was a little speechless. I had raised my children to tell the truth and not lie to me. I told them I can support you with the truth but I can't trust you with a lie. I apologized to the young lady for my daughter's behavior, but I reminded the young lady that she had violated my direct command that we did not have company when I was not home. I offered to take her home since it was already almost 9pm at night and I did not want anything to happen to her on the way home.

When I arrived at her house, I got out of the car to speak with her mother. I apologized, telling her unfortunately my daughter had used some choice words in a conversation with her daughter. I told her that my main concern is that I had expressly asked her daughter not to come over to my home when I'm not at home. I don't mind her coming over, but I do need to be at home before my kids have company over. She seemed to understand and was in agreement. We said good night and suggested we would see each in church on Sunday.

When Sunday came, I went to church. The day was September 8th, my niece's birthday. I had promised all the youth that I was going to take them to Shooters, an all you can eat buffet. When I walked into the church, I noticed there was a hush in the room. The room was quiet. There was definitely something tense in the atmosphere.

"How can you put me on a 30-day probation without having any proof of this lie?"

The pastor of the Youth Ministry called me into his office. When I entered, the young lady's mother was there along with several of the Elders of the church. I was asked to sit down and tell about the incident at my home. After recounting the details of the incident, the mother of the young lady stood up and called me a liar. According to her, I had gone to her home and cursed her out. "You called me everything but a child of God." she insisted.

At that moment, I was dumbfounded. I knew what she was saying was not true. I had thought we had a beautiful conversation as two mothers. I really do not know what transpired since I last saw her. I reiterated that her daughter had come to my home. I didn't go to hers. I told the pastor that my children are my greatest investment and I will protect them with my life if need be.

Then we learned that we would be meeting with the elders of the church, about eleven of them. They reminded me that at the Last Supper Jesus was betrayed by the one who had his head in his bosom. Thoughts flashed through my mind. Many of these people were the ones I had helped in many ways in the past. I didn't want anything except for them to judge fairly in the Spirit. That didn't happen.

We sat there and each one of them had something to say against me that really hurt. They took blessings and twisted their words and made it ugly. I sat there waiting for each person to finish. I did not try to defend myself. It was if God was whispering to me, "Hold your peace. I will fight your battle." All the while, I had this dialogue going on in my mind. I'm telling God, "Yeah, but that's not true. I want to tell her the truth. But, the Holy Ghost restrained me and I held my peace.

The pastor of the ministry is a true prophet of God. I believe God will deal with His prophet. It is not up to me or you to say anything to him or concerning him. So I sat there in disbelief as my pastor put me on a 30-day probation. *How can you put me on a 30-day probation without having any proof of this lie?* I wondered.

Hadn't her daughter shown up uninvited at my house? Hadn't I brought her home to their parents' home and talked to her mother in a loving way? Hadn't I shown compassion by not letting her daughter take the 'L' home late at night although this girl was known to go all over the city of Chicago by herself all times of the night. In the end, it was not my concern or my business how this mother raised her child. I believe God would fight my battle.

My 30-day probation meant I would not be allowed to do any type of ministry in the church. I could attend all the functions but couldn't handle any of my regular duties. I felt falsely accused but so was Jesus. I was just on probation; He was crucified. When I stepped out of my pastor's office that morning, it seems everyone was looking at me. Some were texting about the situation.

When my niece and the other young people found out what had happened, they thought we would no longer be going to Shooters. I assured my niece, "Yes, we are going to go to Shooters. Today is your birthday and this is a family affair. If anyone wants to come along, they are more than welcome. I will take care of the bill."

After the service ended, we left the church and went to Shooters. The kids had a great time. I was laughing, joking and talking. Then about 10 or 15 members from church showed up acting all concerned. "Are you okay?"

"I am fine, perfectly fine." I replied.

The fun continued and the children filled their bellies with food. Everyone seemed to be enjoying themselves. When I got home, I walked into my bedroom and immediately fell to the floor. I began crying uncontrollably. "God I tried to walk upright before you. I tried to be a good example in life. Why are the leaders doing this to me? What did I do? I don't want

this." I was deeply hurt. It felt like I was being at-
tacked by a hornet stinging me over and over again.

Remember, it was September 8th. During that
time, I had three vehicles. I had used them to transport
youth to the ministry on Wednesday and Friday nights
and Sunday mornings. When there were other outings,
I provided rides also. The kids depended on me. I was
not trying to let the kids know how hurt I was. I
prayed to the Lord:

God, if I have wronged anybody in the ministry,
if I have disrespected anybody, most of all, if I have
brought shame to the ministry in any way, please forgive me. Father God, please don't take your Spirit
away from me. Father you know my heart. If I have
not done anything wrong and if my heart is pure, and
you would know, please do not let me not stay on this
probation for 30 days. Break it in the name of Jesus.
Amen"

I laid there. My husband came in and asked
what was wrong but I didn't tell him why I was crying.
I didn't want to sow a seed of criticism against the
church or the men and women of God. But, he knew
something was wrong and insisted I tell him.

When I did, he thought the situation was
messed up. "So what are you going to do?" He asked.

"I don't know."

"Well, I don't think that you should leave now. I
think that you should go through the probation and
then ask God what you should do."

"No! I want to leave now." I responded, reveal-
ing my true feelings and the deep hurt in my heart. "I
went to church every Sunday, every Wednesday and
Friday. If the ministry had an outing I went to support.

I would take the youth if they were singing or dancing. I made sure that they got there."

A few weeks went by and God had not delivered me from my 30-day probation. So I said, "Okay
God, if I have to go through this for 30 days, I'm going
to do it with my head held high."

But, then September 29th rolled around. It was
at our morning service. A friend of my pastor had come
up from Atlanta Georgia. Since he was in town, our
pastor asked him to share the word at service that
morning. I sat in my chair over in the corner praising
the Lord by myself thinking, *Lord, and I worship you now
with lifted hands.*

Our pastor introduced the visiting pastor who
began to preach a message about Elijah and the mantle.
The message was very good, too. Then all of a sudden,
he said, "You, over in the corner." Everybody in the
church turned to see who he was talking to. I looked
around also.

Just then, he continued. "You in that sharp outfit
matching from head to toe. Come up here!"

In my spirit, I said "God don't let them embarrass me again."

I just knew my pastor has told this man all
about me and my 30-day probation. Another dialogue
with the Lord was going on in my head again. I felt so
embarrassed and I did not want to get up. The devil
was telling me "Don't go, don't let them embarrass you.
Just act like you don't know who he's talking to."

But the Holy Spirit urged me to get up and
move forward in obedience. I learned that if you do
nothing else, always walk-in obedience unto the Lord
because obedience is better than sacrifice. By the time I

got up there, I was shaking like a leaf on a tree. I had no idea what he was about to say. I was so nervous.

He looked right at me. "Sister, I don't know you and you don't know me. I don't know why I came here but I know that I need to say something to you urgently. Some witches and warlocks have been meeting concerning you."

"*T*hank you for restoring, saving, and keeping me."

My knees were buckling. I could hear gasps and murmuring in the congregation. Oh, my God!

"There is a contract on your life and the devil is mad at you. He is so angry with you that he is using some of your close friends and maybe even your family members. They have turned their backs on you. I see them meeting to figure out how to get you out of the ministry."

By then, I had lost it. I was on the floor at this point.

"God sent me here just for you to break that contract I am here to break the band of the enemy and shut down those meetings that have been held against you."

He went on. "There were some at the table who did not want to be at the table because you had blessed them. You have paid their car note, helped pay their rent, and bought groceries for their home. You have helped them in whatever way you could. They don't know how they ended up in the meeting but they were drawn into it."

This man was so precise. He spoke of things I had done and ways that I had helped others that my pastor had no idea of. I believe that it was the voice of God when he said, "I have come here to restore you."

When he said 'restore me,' the reservoir on the inside broke. I so needed to hear those words. I needed to be restored and put back in the right place and right standing. My detractors might have met secretly in a back room but I believe God was saying He was going to restore me for the whole world to see. He had built me a platform because He was getting ready to introduce me to the world as a prophet of God.

As the man of God continued to minister to me, God showed me my purpose was for being at this place in this season of life. He continued to pray over me. Then he called my pastor up and asked, "Where is your robe?"

I had already arranged for a young lady to be a nurse for the pastor to make sure that he had everything that he needed for Sunday morning service. She came up and she brought the robe. The pastor said, "Take the robe. It is a representation of the mantle of the prophet."

Then he threw it over my shoulders. When he did that, it felt heavy. I can't explain it. I didn't understand wanting God is heavy but the yoke of the Lord is easy. I thank Jesus that he said, "Receive a double portion."

The gift of the prophet stirred in me. I walked beside a prophet, sat under the teaching of the prophet, worked in his ministry, and I was restored to my rightful place by my pastor after the urging of the minister from Atlanta. My pastor got up, restored me, and then prophesied over my life.

I realize that my struggle was so hard because of the prophetic that had to be birthed in me. I could have stayed at home. I could have left. I could have done a whole lot of things that could have caused me to be bitter. I could have come and not paid my tithes or give my offering. But I came every Sunday and paid my tithes and offerings. I did everything that I was supposed to do. God restored my responsibilities and my ministry.

People came up and hugged me. They said, "I'm so glad God did this for you."

When I got home, I didn't realize that something still hadn't lifted in my spirit. I walked into my bedroom and the Lord spoke to me. He said, "Get the calendar."

I respond, "God I'm tired and I just want to go to sleep. Thank you for restoring, saving, and keeping me. I don't know how it happened but I'm grateful. Thank you Lord."

The Lord spoke again. "Go and get the calendar by your bed." I got the calendar I always keep. "Look at September 8th. That was the day you came into your bedroom, fell on your face, and cried out to me. You asked me to restore you if you had done nothing wrong. You asked me to forgive you for hurting or disrespecting anyone. I sent the answer the very same day that you prayed but the witches and the warlock held up the messenger angel that was dispatched to send your release. I sent warring angels to fight on your behalf."

September 8th until September 29th was exactly 21 days. It was the same number of days that it took for Daniel to receive his answer. (See Daniel 10:12) God said to me, "I am not hard of hearing. I heard you the very first day that you prayed and I sent the answer."

It was time for a praise break! When I heard that I had a dance in my soul. I had asked God to end my probation in less than 30 days and He did it in 21 days! I felt so good. This built my faith in the Lord even more. I will never ever forget this victory as long as I live. There is nothing that will ever be able to snatch it away what God did for me.

God has done so many wonderful things for me, some I didn't even deserve. I hold on to my faith and that lets me know that if I need it and if I walk uprightly before God, He will deliver me. It may not be the way that I want to be delivered but as long as God delivers me, I'm safe.

I remember thinking I wanted to leave the ministry after 30 days. Well now that all this is over and behind me, I don't feel so bad anymore. I decided to stay in the ministry. I was ready to continue on but God was saying to me, "I needed to strip you. I needed to make you vulnerable and more dependent on me. I am stirring those gifts and calling and the anointing on your life to a greater lever. I'm getting ready to take you higher. Little did I know that I would need all the strength and all of the anointing to deal with the next blow that I would receive. After several weeks, things were now quiet at the church.

What Happens When God Says, "Let There Be...!"

CHAPTER 4

The Stirring

Sometimes, when it is time for us to move, we are reluctant because we are too comfortable and complacent. God is like the mother eagle who will ruffle the nest to cause the eaglets to become uncomfortable. When an eagle builds her nest, she builds it at the tops of tall, mature trees or high in the mountains. The nest is well-lined and comfortable for her eggs. After the eggs hatch, the eaglets enjoy a cozy, comfortable place, with food and toys.

"While I was in this ministry, I went through some things but they were all in the Lord's timing."

As the eaglets get older, the mother eagle starts preparing them to go out into the world. She begins to remove the eaglets favorite toys. She takes away the soft furs from rabbits, squirrels and raccoons so the thorns in the bottom of the nest prick the eaglets causing them to flap their wings. This process helps to strengthen their wings. This Is what God had to do to me.

While I was in this ministry, I went through some things but they were all in the Lord's timing. What the Lord was really allowing me to discover was that my season in it that ministry was drawing to a close. My purpose in that ministry under a mighty prophet of God was for the gift of discernment and the prophetic to be stirred in my life. When the mantle was placed upon my shoulders, I received what the Lord wanted me to receive. Sitting under the anointing of the prophet, traveling with him in ministry, receiving the laying on of hands, and teaching under the anointing was preparing me for the next level in ministry. I couldn't see the whole plan that God had laid out for my life so I got comfortable.

I forgot my prayer to leave the ministry after my probationary period was over. The negative experiences I went through happened not to kill me but to strengthen my wings for flight. When I was a young girl, I remember when my mother spanked me. She often said something I did not understand for the life of me: "This is going to hurt me more than it hurts you!"

Are you kidding me? I figured if it is going to hurt you and me, just don't do it. But that reasoning didn't help at all. I had to bear down and take it like a champ. So, God allowed me to experience the pricks in the ministry that my wings could be strengthened.

After a few weeks had gone bye I began to notice some of my friends being distant with me. I didn't know or understand why. I was not sure what was happening in our relationships but I was desperately trying to hold on to relationships God was breaking me away from. My friends were moving on without me. The phone calls stopped and there were no longer invitations to different events and functions.

I found myself crying sometimes. I complained to my husband. I didn't know what I had done to cause this. My husband spoke this truth to me. "Well, what makes you think that it's not God separating you from them?"

Why? I wondered. Then a thousand memories flashed through my mind. I saw myself with no friends, being alone all the time with nobody to talk to. No more movies, picnics, playing cards, and board games. My children are not able to visit them anymore. I was just beating myself up, crying, and wondering out loud: *what have I done now?*

A spirit of embarrassment began to come over me. I immediately started shaking that spirit of me and putting it out of my mind. So, what if the phone calls had stopped coming?

One Saturday morning, our Pastor had to preach at a church on South Indiana Avenue at 11am in the morning. I was happy to get up early to be at church, but deep down inside I also wanted to see my friends. To my surprise, none of them showed up. The ache in my heart shook me almost to the core. The service started and it was a great service. The Lord moved and truly blessed the people. I was glad to be a part of it all.

When the service was over. I was heading to my car when an Evangelist stopped me and asked if she could give me a word from the Lord.

"Yes, you can," I replied.

The Evangelist began to prophesy to me. She told me that God had placed a heavy anointing on my life. The anointing God was placing on my life would be heavy and cutting edge. This anointing would cause me to walk a lonely road of life. The ministries to be birthed through me will have me traveling. My travels would require me to have light baggage.

That reminded me of this verse: "Wherefore seeing we also are compassed about with so great a cloud of witnesses, let us lay aside every weight, and the sin which doth so easily beset us, and let us run with patience the race that is set before us. (Hebrew 12:1)

Many compare this text to a runner who has to make sure that everything attached to him is lightweight, where the wind from his speed cannot slow him down by getting under his clothing. On the other hand, I look at the eagle. The eagle can fly higher than any bird in the sky. It is majestic!

The eagle goes through a process called feaking to keep their beaks and talons clean and groomed. When too much keratin (a bony structure) grows on the talons and beak of an eagle, the eagle will rub their talons and beaks against hard rocks to clean and keep them sharpened.

Like the eagle, we must be vigilant to clean our mouths since life and death come from the tongue. This is necessary for survival. The mouth must be dull to the world but sharp for the Spirit. I needed to be a buffer for the ministry.

The evangelist who prophesied over me said that it is not so much that friends were leaving but that God was removing distractions and weights from me. The places God was getting ready to send me were not places they were ready to go. Then, she encouraged me and assured me that I would not be lonely and there would be no void in me.

I needed to hear those words from the Lord. Those words from God prepared me for what I was about to encounter. God was making my nest uncomfortable and exposing my complacency. Friends were falling away. The lies continued among some of them. Then rumors started that I was saying negative things about my leaders. Those whom I once considered friends were not talking to me. So who could I confide in?

The pastoral team of a husband and wife were the overseers of the ministry and they were located in Michigan. The apostle's wife had a powerful and life changing ministry on Tuesday called "L.I.V.E." which stood for Living Intentionally Victoriously Eternally. Every Tuesday I would pack me and my daycare babies in my van and we would head out to L.I.V.E. ministry. I had been attending for about two years and I simply loved it. That would soon be cut off from me as well.

One Sunday morning, I was at our church and I needed to get something from the stockroom next to the ladies washroom. The walls separating the two rooms were paper thin. While in the stockroom, I overheard a loud conversation going on in the washroom. I heard my name being mentioned and I overheard the leaders saying that it's time for her to go. They were discussing my tithes and offering and the building fund I was sowing into per our leaders request. They got so petty. I heard them talking about my shoes, hair, and nails. Why? This was truly stirring my nest and it was very uncomfortable for me.

The time had finally come. We had services on Friday at 7pm. Around 4 pm, my phone rang. and I saw it was our pastor calling. I answered thinking he was calling to give me instructions for the evening service. I was not prepared to hear what he said to me.

"I needed some kind of answer from the Lord for me and for my children."

"Elder, I have sought the Lord, taken counsel with my elders, and we think it is best if you were no longer a member of this ministry."

My heart skipped a beat, I couldn't breathe, I was gasping for air. But, I stood firm. I didn't yell and I didn't try to defend myself or ask why. Instead I said, "If I have caused this ministry any type of shame or embarrassment, please forgive me."

I think this shocked him as well as it did me. I couldn't believe what was coming out of my mouth. Then, after a brief moment of silence he said, "I am not talking about the children not coming."

Mind you, I was bringing three car loads of young men and women every Friday and Sunday and sometimes on Wednesday evening. They were dancers, actors, gangbangers who were turning their lives around in God. I had to quickly say, "Are you serious?" I was thinking, *do you really believe I would allow my children to stay or go anywhere where I am not wanted?* Most of them were family members, children whom I have been in their lives from birth?

I thanked the pastor for his impartation. "I have received a great deal from you but it is time to move on and my children go where I go."

That whole weekend I did not tell the children I was not allowed to go to the church. First, I was embarrassed to tell them. Second, I was disappointed. After telling them time and again that the church was a place of hope for all sinners and believers, how could I tell them that I had been asked to leave the ministry?

I woke up Tuesday morning and headed to L.I.V.E. ministry. I felt a connection there and I needed some kind of answer from the Lord for me and for my children. As soon as I made it to the church, the presence of the Lord was high and the anointing was definitely in the room. I began to praise the Lord when all of a sudden the pastor of the church looked up and acknowledged my former pastor coming into the sanctuary. My heart skipped two beats. My nerves were all balled up inside my stomach and my knees were trembling.

The first thing that came to mind was he was here to tell them that I was excommunicated from the church. I was about to be the most embarrassed person in the world. But, all he did was set down in the back of the church. I cried through the whole service. I was on pins and needles sitting there.

Once the service was over, I immediately got my babies to leave. My ex-pastor stepped into the aisle and gave me a hug. It seemed as if he wanted to say something but the words never came. And I was okay with that. I couldn't wait to leave. The one good thing that did come out of the service was that God told me to just to continue to show Him in my life.

By the time 7:00pm rolled around, everybody at the church already knew about the phone call. But a strange thing occurred late that night. One of my closest friends called me to tell me to apologize for her role in the whole witch hunt. She knew the things she heard people say about me were untrue, but she couldn't say anything. Her lips were frozen shut. Another friend called and said that she never thought it would go this far. The one thing that our spiritual mom and dad had taught us was love. But, all that mattered now was how to tell the three car loads of young people that I was leaving the ministry where God had been transforming their lives day by day.

My son, daughter, and I were the drivers that picked them up for church. That day, instead of going to the church, I made a detour and took them out for pizza. My nephew who is quite sharp and doesn't miss a thing looked at me and asked, "Auntie, what's wrong?"

I just looked at him and no words came out of my mouth. Finally, we made it to Pizza Hut. While waiting for our pizza, I prayed and asked God for his guidance and the right words to say. The first thing I wanted them all to know is that they had not done anything wrong. God had chosen another path for me to go on. The direction God was leading me to was not at the ministry we all were attending. I told them that I had been asked to leave the ministry but that they could stay if they chose too.

My nephew, the one who asked me what was wrong quickly chimed in. "Auntie! Are you joking with us? If it wasn't for you Auntie we would ride out on them!!!"

Then this young man made the statement I will never forget: "If they put you out of the church and you are always doing good and helping people, what do you think they will do to us gangbangers or think about us who don't walk, talk and act like them? Auntie, you are our pastor and wherever you are we are covered."

These young people followed me and I am happy to report that today some are police, city workers, physical therapists, fathers, husbands. We left the ministry, but we left with our head held high.

Three weeks later, I received a phone call from a couple of the members still there with whom I maintained a great relationship. They called to tell me that they went to the church on Sunday morning, there was a pad-lock on the door. There were no signs or explanation on the door. They called but nobody answered or returned their calls. The next Sunday, they discovered the ministry had been closed, shut down for whatever reason. I was speechless! All I could hear in my spirit was the word *Ichabod* meaning without glory or the glory has departed. Selah.

What Happens When God Says, "Let There Be...!"

CHAPTER 5

The Womb

"God had a plan for me even when I was an unborn child"

"For you created my inmost being; you knit me together in my mother's womb. I praise you because I am fearfully and wonderfully made; your works are wonderful, I know that full well. My frame was not hidden from you when I was made in the secret place, when I was woven together in the depths of the earth. Your eyes saw my unformed body; all the days ordained for me were written in your book before one of them came to be." (Psalms 139:13-16)

When I read these verses, I often think about the virtuous woman who gave birth to me. It was her womb that God used to house me and shape me into the masterpiece He had already designed in heaven. Her womb could have very well been my tomb or sepulcher, small room or monument, cut in rock or built of stone, in which a dead person is laid or buried. But, by the grace of God He said "Let there Be!!!" And there was me.

I am dedicating this chapter of my memoir to my mother, my earthly rock here on earth. She played such a major role in my development. She made sure that I had everything I needed even while I was in her womb, stretching her stomach, causing her uncomfortable pains, irritability, and bruising her on the inside. She ate food that she normally wouldn't eat. She took pills when she was not sick to keep me healthy just in case she couldn't get a meal. She went to the doctor when it wasn't convenient for her, allowing strangers to probe her body. She sacrificed all this and more for me.

Why? Because her womb was a designated Holy place. She couldn't afford the prettiest clothes to fit her stomach while I laid comfortable in her womb. She worried about how she would dress, feed, and take care of me. Yet, she took time to minister to the rest of the family in her roles of wife, mother, and daughter.

Let me introduce you to her. Proverb 31:10-31 describes just a small portion of who this giant of a woman was. She was only 5 feet tall, weighing in at 250 pounds. She was a classy lady of elegance with creativity all down on the inside of her. Her talents were sewing and baking. With her sewing talent, she was able to make clothes for her children. When money was tight, her creativity soared.

---

*"**B**ut when it pleased God, who separated me from my mother's womb, and called me by his grace, **to** reveal his Son in me, that I might preach him among the heathen; immediately I conferred not with flesh and blood."*

Back in the day, from 1890 to around 1960, flour and animal feed would be stored in feed sacks of khaki and pastels. My mother collected these sacks and made cute dresses. Then she would starch and iron them. She would take our socks and embellish them with pretty lace from the 5 and 10 cent store. She would sew on our socks to match the lace on our dresses. Then she would make matching hair bands for our hair.

For my brothers and Dad, she made shirts. People also brought her material to make car and couch covers. With the scraps, she made quilts to keep us warm.

My mother's cooking skills were also exceptional. She was famous for her famous homemade biscuits and pies. Some caucasian families often paid her to cook for their family gatherings.

When it came to fishing, my mother had skills. When she went fishing everybody wanted to tag along because she knew exactly when and where to catch the best fish. If you ask me, she sure was an all-in-one resource who surely was a virtuous woman.

She also was a pro at gardening. Mother had one of the best vegetable gardens you ever wanted to see. She grew all types of vegetables and knew how to prune fruit trees. At harvest time, she canned fruits and vegetables for the winter months.

We may have been poor financially, but we were rich with family relationships and spirit. Tears cloud my eyes and joy fills my heart to know that I came from a strong woman of courage who had such a deep love for her children. When I was much younger, I remember that my mother got real sick and they had to take her to the doctor. She went kicking and screaming because she did not want to go. The doctor examined her and discovered she was badly dehydrated. She was suffering from significant weight loss because she had been missing meals or hardly eating enough food. Apparently, she was sacrificing her food for us. If we asked for more because we saw it on the stove, she would give it to us even though she had not eaten. She wanted to make sure my dad and brothers had food since they worked in the fields.

As I got older and heard these heroic stories about my mother, our bond became stronger. While she carried me, hidden in the secret place of her womb, God was using that time to knit my life together before He revealed me to the world. The Hebrew word for womb is *racham* and it is translated as mercy and compassion. In the Greek, womb is *koilia*, the place where a baby is conceived and nourished. (Darrow, M. 2020). My mother's womb was a nourishing place of fertility and potential for my development. She housed me in secret until the finished product was ready to be presented.

I am the 9th child of my mother and father. She often said to me that there was something unusual about me. My dad thought something was wrong with me. I thought and did things differently. I didn't realize it then but God was calling me from the time I was in my mother's womb. I like the verse in Galatians 1:15-16 that says, *"But when it pleased God, who separated me from my mother's womb, and called me by his grace, to reveal his Son in me, that I might preach him among the heathen; immediately I conferred not with flesh and blood."*

God entrusted me to my mother. That is why I trust this woman who housed me in her womb while God sculpted me. I know that I am fearfully, wonderfully made for a divine purpose driven life. Just like the nameless, virtuous woman Proverbs introduces us to in chapter 31, I could not be more proud of the talented and valuable woman whom I call MOTHER.

EPILOGUE

EPILOGUE

In this book I have shared with you some of my unfolding experiences according to what God has spoken over my life. I shared the story of the two pastors that had hurt me the most because I thought it necessary since it laid a foundation in me that nothing else could have. I never thought church leaders could hurt you in church. As a young girl, I grew up in church but I was shielded from all that grown-up business and things going on behind the scenes. Unless you were really a busybody, you might never know. As a result, I was protected from a lot of hurts in the church.

But that is when I was a child. Now I am an adult, married with two beautiful children. I have discovered that church can be a tough place. I have gotten hurt by the very people that I trusted with my heart and with my life. But would you know that we have never stopped loving each other in spite of all the things that have gone on in ministry?

Now I realized that every pain, every hurt was building me, forcing me to exercise spiritual muscles that were on the inside of me. The more I was persecuted, the stronger I became. It was building character in me. I was growing in patience, long-suffering, temperance, joy, faith, and love.

The Bible tells us that love covers a multitude of sins. (1 Peter 4:8) I Corinthians chapter 13 describes love in all its fullness. We learn that love is not selfish;

it suffers long and is kind. Love does not envy; love vaunteth not itself and is not puffed up. Love does not behave itself unseemly. It does not seek its own and is not easily provoked. Love thinks no evil and it does not rejoice in iniquity but rejoices in truth. Love bears all things, believes all things, and endures all things love never fails.

I believe that because my heart was full of love, the enemy could not penetrate my emotions. I understand now the necessity of enduring what I did under the leadership of the pastors I served. One of my favorite pastors has now gone on to heaven to receive his reward. We all remained the best of friends.

Another pastor is still like a father to me. He was still there for me even though I thought I would lose all of that. I later found out that the other pastor that put me out of the church had been pressured to do that. It is unfortunate that an angry mob of people can cause you to do things that are not godly. But again, it was necessary for what I needed from him. He made a deposit in me and that mantle of the prophet was the greatest reward I received-- speaking the oracles of God's word.

It is so amazing when you witness a prophecy come to pass. I am blessed to have testimony after testimony of how God's words can change a person's life. I see how it has changed my life. Although I no longer minister under my old pastors, I minister alongside him and his wife. We are good friends. I have learned that no matter what you go through, when God speaks over your life, it will unfold in time. Sometimes that unfolding is painful like a woman giving birth after carrying a baby for 9 months. Just as the pain of labor prepares a woman to deliver a baby into the world, God has used the pain of struggles to unfold a life of purpose and power in me.

Darrow. (2020, February 24). Your Mother's Womb: Where God Shapes You for Life! Retrieved November 08, 2020, from http://darrowmillerandfriends.com/2020/02/24/your-mothers-womb-where-god-shapes-you-for-life/

ABOUT THE AUTHOR

Associate Pastor Dollie Sherman is a devoted and loving wife, mother and grandmother to her husband of 41 years, two adult children and one grand-daughter. She fosters to raise her nephew and God-grandson.

Pastor Dollie is a member of Progressive Life-Giving Word Cathedral where Apostle Donald Alford is Senior Pastor and Associate Pastor Lady Gloria Alford. Pastor Dollie teaches Sunday school, teaches in James Benjamin Alford Bible Institute. She served as Director over Empowerment Sessions and PSOM (Progressive School of Ministry) worship committee coordinator. Her ministry is under the umbrella of Progressive Fellowship for Kingdom Builders. She serves in many capacities in her local church and works closely with Lady Gloria Alford on the women's auxiliary Ladies of Elegance.

Pastor Sherman, Proprietor and CEO of Kidz Cozy Corner Learning Center, operating in Chicago, Illinois over 30 years, has been known to minister the love of Jesus Christ to every family that patronizes her business. Many families have found her wise counseling and mentoring to be a peace in the midst of the storm. Several parents have given their lives to the Lord. She is founder of Vessels unto Honor Women's Ministry dedicated and geared toward helping broken women and men from all walks of life. Without-stretched hands, she ministers to the needs of the community by providing food, clothing and other vital resources as needed. She provides prayer and counseling to single mothers, fathers, and married couples. She has a passion for aiding men and women in discovering their purpose in God.

Pastor Sherman holds an Associate Degree in Early Childhood Education and a Bachelor Degree in Urban Ministry. She holds a Bachelor Degree in Applied Behavioral Science from National Lewis University. She's currently pursuing her Master's Degree in Early Childhood Administration. She served as the Vice-President over the Western Suburb Daycare Alliance for SEIU. She's an Engagement Specialist and outreach coordinator for Austin Coming Together Organization. She's a Restorative Justice Circle Keeper and conference pastor to many other women ministries world-wide. She's also the author of a newly published book entitled What Happens when God Says, "Let There…Be!".

Pastor Sherman has conducted many workshops for local churches and women ministries throughout the United States. God has given her divine revelation on such topics as Spiritual Warfare, Virtuous Women becoming God's Queen, A touch from the Potter's hand, Tithes and Offering as a weapon against the Devil and countless others. The Holy Spirit reveals the secrets of men's hearts as she ministers to God's people. She has ministered to NFL Football mothers and wives conference gatherings in downtown Chicago on the Magnificent Mile, Pastor Sherman's soul desire is to carry out the commission of God for her life.

What Happens When God Says, "Let There Be...!"